TOGETHER

ECE TEMELKURAN

Together

10 Choices for a Better Now

4th ESTATE • London

4th Estate
An imprint of HarperCollins*Publishers*
1 London Bridge Street
London SE1 9GF

www.4thEstate.co.uk

HarperCollins*Publishers*
1st Floor, Watermarque Building, Ringsend Road
Dublin 4, Ireland

First published in Great Britain in 2021 by 4th Estate

1

Copyright © Ece Temelkuran 2021

Set in Sabon LT Std
Printed and bound in Great Britain by
CPI Group (UK) Ltd, Croydon

MIX
Paper from
responsible sources
FSC™ C007454

This book is produced from independently certified FSC™ paper
to ensure responsible forest management.

For more information visit: www.harpercollins.co.uk/green

To little Valentino
I dare to promise you.

Contents

A few words before we begin:
A talisman for us, for now

Since we can't cry it off, we laugh: two determined headless chickens clucking into the apocalypse. The world is coming to an end, and for the last ten minutes, we have been meticulously trying to separate the plastic lining of our envelopes from the paper.

It is another early morning in the late spring of 2020, only a few weeks into lockdown, one week after a massive earthquake rocked Zagreb. And now, there is a dust cloud hanging over the whole city. We are two women of the same age standing on Marticeva Street, by the recycling bins, holding our half-torn bubble-wrap envelopes and shaking from our guffaws together even though we don't know each other.

But for just a split second, our eyes meet and we see each other and ourselves: our hair messed up, Covid masks crooked, and we are sorting our garbage into the appropriate bins to give us even a tiny bit of control over our garbage-like times since our latex-gloved hands are banned from fixing anything else. Pyramids and revolutions, symphonies and space travel, quantum physics and the Mona Lisa and here we are, at the start of the twenty-first century, looking like the garbage of human history.

Our sickening laughter is there to choke the all too human question of our times: Is this all we can be now? All we can do?

'What do we do now?'

During 2019, I was expected to answer that question after almost every talk I delivered, in countless different theatres in countless different countries. After *How to Lose a Country* was published, I spent almost the whole year speaking about the logic of the political machine that had created all the confusion, fear and desperation we found ourselves suffering. No country is immune to the paralysing political and moral plague of our times, I was saying. But by the time I managed to convince the relaxed Western audiences that this new type of fascism was waging a global war against basic human reasoning, my predictions were already coming true. Each time I finished a talk, for a brief moment, the same heavy silence filled the room right before the Q&A began. In that lead-like stillness, I eventually understood, many were trying to make a crucial choice: 'Shall I ask for the way out of this invasive insanity or shall I just go out and have a drink to forget?' After all, many of us thought that the choices we had so far been provided with by today's world were rarely more meaningful than tearing bubble wrap out of paper envelopes. Or they were terrifyingly massive, like all-out revolution. The vast space in between where real life happened was rarely the issue. And in that real life a period of history was coming to end, but it rather felt like humankind was collapsing altogether.

All status quos have the magical ability of deceiving the masses into believing that when the system collapses everything else will collapse with it.

All systems act this way, like fearful ancient sailors: they warn that once you sail into uncharted waters, you will fall off the edge of the world. This is what we're told is happening to us now. The economic and political system that we have built has reached its limits and, while it begins to fall, it threatens to drag us down with it. Any choice we make seems as ineffective as a bucket bailing water from a filling hull. The enormity of the chaos deceives us into believing that whatever we do is too small. And finally we tend to forget that our kind is in fact able to reinvent itself through even the smallest of things.

It is not clear from where I stand whether it is a child's instinct to be gentle with small objects or the learned disgust that keeps her from grabbing them fully. But Zeyno, a five-year-old, is collecting things on a deserted shore of the Greek island Kalymnos in the summer of 2019. She holds them up with the tip of her fingers and runs back to the parasol. But once each item is safely stored she resumes her slow walk, scanning the ground.

As her endeavour becomes so clearly persistent, two middle-aged women begin following her from opposite sides of the beach. Their lazy gait carefully conceals genuine curiosity as they pretend Zeyno's parasol *just happens* to be on their way. They stop to glance at the mysterious pile. 'Pieces of plastic,' one of them says. 'Ah, she's collecting garbage,' responds the other. They exchange that mournful smile adults give when met with a display of enthusiasm. Zeyno, like a mother squirrel that has detected danger, runs back to protect the nest. Trying to catch her breath, she delivers a determined speech about how plastic is very, very bad for 'mother earth' and how garbage can be turned into 'art', yes it can. After giving Zeyno an approving pat on the head, the women walk back to their parasols. Almost at the same second, though, they stop, pick up a piece of litter from the sand and return to contribute to the little girl's collection. Instead of getting back to sunbathing they too begin to scan the sand. An unexpected midday poetry sweeps them along and they remember: Even in today's garbage-like times it is our inherent disposition to create beauty that has sustained our kind each time a system ended up in the dustbin of history. And during each collapse, despite those who believed that this was the end of it all, this essence of our kind has been the reason to renew our faith in humanity.

When I was Zeyno's age, I was still able to hear the mute language of things. There was a drawer in our home that acted as the final waiting room for small objects that were no longer of use. The decision on their destiny was constantly postponed: pens with annoying temperaments that might work one day, gift package ribbons waiting to be used in emergency present situations, the rusting keys of long-gone doors, partially dried-out lipsticks, a broken hand mirror with anthracite veins, peeling plastic combs and all the et cetera of our life that could no longer claim their own places in our home. They all lay there waiting for my mother's next jettisoning-our-life moment. But their moaning, the disturbing cry of the fallen that only I could hear, was unbearable to my ears.

One day, I started sticking all these poor things together, a rescue operation of sorts. Gradually they became strange talismans that hung in my room. As they were placed back in the world as parts of a whole they were able to speak again.

Together is no different. The book is a talisman bringing together all those small things about our kind that we don't remember forgetting in the drawers of humanity. Only by mending them together can we remind ourselves how and why humans have managed to survive up until now, and why we have kept choosing to have faith in ourselves.

As you read my words, you will see seemingly insignificant moments, broken images, partially dried-out dreams, unbuilt cities and all the et cetera of the world. This is a new human story made up from the bits and pieces of the broken images of our kind.

This talisman of a book is about ten real-life choices for people like us, the ones who bother to read and write books such as this. These choices are not to be made in some unknown future but now, exactly where and when we need them. *Together* is for us to choose us, once again.

To some, these choices may sound too delicate to match the brutality of our times. Yet, *all things of value are fragile*; the beautiful, the humane and the true. And when all that is fragile is mended to form a solid story of our kind, only then it wouldn't sound strange if I suddenly say, 'I believe in you.'

But to create a new and a better story for our kind I need you. I need you to make a choice, and to make it now.

Now is a devastating word.

Now is the image of a little girl who freezes in mid-step when it is her turn to jump over the skipping rope. As the others shout – 'Now! Jump now!' – the rope starts to look like the tongue of a snake. Its every lick of the ground enunciates to the girl that it is always too late.

People like you and me are like that girl now, frozen in mid-step. Some of us keep asking for hope or encouragement to jump in and some of us have already given up, have left the playground altogether. Fewer and fewer people are asking the way out of the global madness. Many of us are silently deciding only to seek our personal safety. *Now* feels like it might be too late. Too late even to ask the question of what we do now.

Yet, now is the time to choose to believe: to believe that we are better than headless chickens, that we are destined for beauty and that we don't need to wait for better times for hope. The right moment is ... Now!

And, if you choose to believe, I promise, we can jump over that damn rope of time together.

1

Choose faith over hope

In 2019, my irritation at the ever-present question 'So where, then, is hope?' became so self-destructive that by the end of the year I was reacting to it sarcastically. I fantasised about handing the next person who dared ask me the question a menu for Restaurant Hope. I pictured a quaint brasserie serving a main course of Back to Our Senses Stew. Diners would be offered a bowl of Democracy served in a rich sauce of Sensible, Grown-up Politicians, with all the Global Turmoil evaporated off. But, of course, where there is sarcasm there is always a wrongly healed heartbreak.

It is already common knowledge: My country, Turkey, is a difficult place to be. For years, only a small number of people have managed to do enough to change the bloody course of events. And during those long years, the rest of Turkey has been asking for hope. I have heard the word too many times from those who did not do nearly enough, so many times that the word itself started to sound to me like an emotional crutch for those who just didn't dare to stand tall.

Today, the Western world that has claimed, since the eighteenth century, to be a safe haven for the individual, the free thinker, is also becoming a difficult place to be. Europeans and Americans are learning to feel not so much like individuals protected by laws and moral codes, but more like guinea pigs in a massive experiment to measure our capacity to endure unending political and moral challenges. The West is also experiencing how paralysing it is to witness tragedies when they are mixed with absurdities, served with ruthless lies by clownish and at times Darth Vader-like political figures. We all know now the numbing effect of being bombarded with shamelessness from the upper echelons of politics and how it energises ruthlessness in daily life. Immorality wraps itself in a cultural and a political identity, baptising itself as 'the free choice of real people'. And as we witnessed during the pandemic in 2020, this insanity can cost hundreds of thousands of human lives.

The only upside of this worldwide political and moral maze is that now we are in it together, no country is spared, and so we must hold onto one another as we look for the exit. But my heart aches whenever I hear people in other countries, newly introduced to the maze, making the exact same mistakes while asking about hope.

However, there is a much bigger problem than my irritation. Since these confusing times provide us with the ugliest and lowest representations of humankind, a dangerous thought sooner or later comes to the surface: 'Are humans essentially rotten?' As this virulent question becomes more common, it starts damaging our essential reason to exist and to act. It is like the scene in Luc Besson's film *The Fifth Element* when Leeloo, who is supposed to save the world, learns about the brutality of humans and decides they don't deserve saving. And in our case a passionate kiss from Bruce Willis may not be enough to convince us otherwise. A new generation is growing up questioning whether humans deserve to exist as much as other species do. And it is not easy to persuade them of the opposite when the immoral representatives of humankind and their frantic devotees are plumbing the depths of what we can morally bear.

During a talk at the Edinburgh Festival, I tried my best to do some of this persuading. After telling the audience that hope was too weak a word to do the job and that only our inherent determination to create beauty would save us, I thought I was done. Yet a woman with beautiful grey hair approached me after the talk. A cross was hanging from her neck.

'Don't be impatient with them when they ask for hope,' she said. She did not waste time exchanging niceties as writers and readers normally do. She jumped right in. So I did the same.

'I am ...' I said, 'Actually, the whole world is crumbling and we can do more than ask for hope. And what if there is no hope? Do we just lie down and accept our fate? Or, a more dangerous question: what if there is hope? Are they ready to do what it takes?'

She gently caught my hand in the air, compassionately but firmly, as if rescuing a bird that has flown indoors. She looked like one of those rare women who had earned the lines on her face. 'They mean something else when they speak of hope.' She laid my hand on the table as if trusting me with a secret: 'Think about faith.' She must have seen me looking at her cross with a know-it-all smirk, so she added with a forgiving smile, 'Not the religious kind.'

So I did.

'OK, this is what we do. We stand in the middle of the terminal and we spin around on the spot with our eyes closed. Once we stop, we'll open our eyes, and whichever city we see on the adverts in front of us, we are going there.'

This was a dare that I came up with in the central bus station in Ankara, the Turkish capital, in the spring of 1991 with a group of friends all equally bored of our law training. The challenge would be to make it back home from wherever we ended up. We only had enough money to reach the destination; the rest was up to our survival skills, fed by our limitless self-confidence. After our fateful spinning, our destination was set: Trabzon, a town on the Black Sea close to the border with the Soviet Union, which had collapsed that very year. And like that, less than twelve hours from the moment we started to spin, we were wandering idly through a hastily erected new flea market that the locals called the 'Russian Bazaar'. This was where a fallen regime turned the everyday items of a people into souvenirs of failed Socialism.

Since the fall of the USSR, the medals that people had died and killed for had become cool accessories for university students' coats – and God knows what happened to all those old gas masks. In between the bulky thermometers, rugged furs and military belts there were ceramic earrings missing a pair, decorated teapots with tea leaves still inside and saucers without cups. The turn of history was so sudden there hadn't even been time to wash the dishes. The bazaar was unusually silent, not only because the sellers were still new to the free-market economy, but also because they were now tasked with simply selling their lives.

A too-close breath tickled the back of my neck:
'Hey Natasha, sex?'

The greasy whisper of a young man made me want to rub my ear clean. Meeting his lusty eyes, I jumped back and answered in haste, 'I am not Russian.' The apology was as quick, 'Oh, sorry sister.' Natasha was a common name for Russian women on sale, and I was lucky enough to be the daughter of a still officially viable ideology – Capitalism. I was off-market. I was safe.

The women in the market suddenly became inseparable from the items laid out on the tables, and their price tags were now visible. The silence turned from melancholic to disgusting. While 'Socialism is dead' carnivals were getting under way among Western think-tanks, and some business-minded bandits were turning themselves into fledgling Russian oligarchs, there were also men at markets like this one, in the countries surrounding the former USSR, who sold nothing more than a single little box of caviar and a bottle of Russian vodka. Eyes totally blank, they smoked cheap cigarettes, and wore Marxist moustaches that had turned overnight into period drama make-up. Those who witnessed these days would remember that the one thing more devastating than the Death of a Salesman was his forced premature birth.

'Capitalism needs a reset,' declared the front page of the *Financial Times*.

The paper was almost pleading with those negligent deities in charge of the money. Although the wise men of the free-market economy have been talking about Capitalism hitting a dead end for years in their closed summits, the public announcement was still earth-shaking. As if by speaking the very word 'Capitalism', the paper was admitting that it was only a finite economic and political model, not the natural state of the world. It sounded like a confession from Capitalism itself: there is life beyond the model, or at least beyond this savage version of it.

Today, although more and more people realise that we are witnessing the collapse of an economic model, the question might still sound surreal. But what would a flea market of collapsed Capitalism look like? Alongside the billions of utterly unnecessary items, I bet there would be piles of self-help books on individual success and equally big piles of books saying it is OK to fail. The two biggest piles, though, would be of books attempting to reinvent hope, and ones on hopeless dystopias. In my mind's eye, I can see us smiling in despair while looking at these two heaps of souvenirs that almost cancel each other out. And we, the people, would look like – well, pretty much how we look today: the victims of a failed project, lost and confused. Maybe only our Instagram filters would keep us looking better than those former USSR citizens in Russian bazaars. But sooner or later we would have to recognise that what turns humans to rags and tatters is the loss of direction, and our ability to believe that we are competent enough to find a new one. It is the very thing that today makes us ask 'Are humans rotten and therefore redundant?' That makes us lose our faith in humankind.

Faith is the only word that can at once accommodate all those concepts that seem to be in pieces: self-esteem, confidence, trust. The word faith, however, requires us to walk the line between poetry and the foggy realm of theology. Both fields require a different vocabulary than this little book of mine can offer. Faith sounds religious because for thousands of years it has been the custom to make God or gods the North Star of our ability to believe. It has been easier to allow mysticism to monopolise the concept of faith, because our talent for believing is too terrifying to be placed in the mundane. The word itself has a dangerous, almost explosive potential. It has therefore always been safer to wrap this limitless power of ours in the divine and remove the source of it somewhere outside our mortal selves.

The Left has often kept itself distant from the concept, even sneered at it as I did at that woman's cross in Edinburgh, because – besides any philosophical reasons – the word faith has a habit of getting out of hand. It creates a dangerous relationship among mortals, turning them into blind followers and – not rarely – beasts of cruelty. Only when we acknowledge the idea of God as our own invention – that is, something impossible to contaminate and therefore the safest intermediary between ourselves and others in this heartless world

– might we manage to accommodate faith into this mundane reality of ours.

I will leave God in the realm of poetry and theology and, instead, provide something closer to the annoying shake we give someone falling asleep in the snow of cynicism and depression that feels so warm. Here's another dare to test these deliberations on faith in the human, this time in a holy place. It is the Basilica Palatina di Santa Barbara, in the ancient Italian town of Mantua.

It is almost impossible for anyone coming from the Sunni Muslim world to imagine giving a speech about a political book in a holy place. If you are a woman who is supposed to enter the mosque from a side door, trying to hide yourself from the male-dominated congregation, it is an especially strange feeling to enter a church and be welcomed at the altar. Yet here I am, in this sixteenth-century basilica, dazed by the echo of my voice when I say 'I believe not in God, but in humans.'

Even when I say we don't need religion to have faith and trust in each other, the resonance wraps my words in a certain air of divinity. The silence turns from that of the ordinary curiosity of listeners to the joyful oneness of a congregation as I mention the words 'faith in humankind' and 'the beauty of the human'. I hear sighs of relief.

It is Italy, after all: when the rest of the Western world did not have a clue about political and moral insanity, the Italians had Silvio Berlusconi, who was more entertaining than Boris Johnson and far more dangerous than Donald Trump. They were the first nation in Europe to experience the sharp turn of history, while the rest of the Western world thought it was a temporary Mediterranean craziness. They are tired of the shame of being represented by the worst of them – which, despite their cooler climates, is now also the case for the most mature democracies and most economically formidable countries.

Tear-filled eyes and full smiles meet me when I come down from the altar, which for an instant makes me feel like an impostor televangelist. But as my cynicism fades, I realise that this is what happens when words are used as a cardiac massage to reactivate the human heart that thousands of years ago invented gods – and before that, faith itself. This is the only human mechanism that can cure our deep sense of failure and the self-hate that follows. Because it is there, still ticking, even after hundreds of disasters and thousands of tyrants, whenever it has seemed as though our humanity has been abandoned. It is not a directionless 'Yes, we can', but rather a reminder to people of their ability to find a new direction – and the necessity to have faith in their own power. The convenience of the word 'faith' comes from the fact that we know it already, and that it requires no proof and cannot be refuted.

'Do you have hope for your country?' a journalist asked the Iranian actress Golshifteh Farahani while her homeland was once again resisting Islamic totalitarianism.

For a split second she fell silent, as if the question annoyed her. Then she said, 'I don't have hope for fire to burn. I don't have hope for water to flow. Human nature is to be free. Iran will be free.'

It is understandable that such a brave woman, who left her country in order to realise her passion, should think that freedom is an integral part of the human character. However, if you see a wide enough variety of people, you realise that it is in fact difficult to prove that humans have such high merits. Once it is based on such elevated expectations, faith in humankind becomes a shaky theory. It is not the radical evil that hibernates in humankind that makes me say this; it is our ability so often to be maddeningly banal, to be blank and meek. Our understanding of human nature cannot be limited to actual humans, whether they are maddeningly ordinary or amazingly inspiring. 'There must be something else,' says my need to believe in the human, and therefore to believe in you.

* * *

'Oh, it's one of the most popular attractions in the city.' The lovely volunteer at the bookstall at the Festival of Ideas tells me about a tour called 'Unbuilt Bristol'. She gives me a flyer that reads, 'Join local historian Eugene Byrne for a walking tour of things that aren't there.' Byrne, who wrote a book with the same title, takes you around the city to tell you about all the projects that never came to fruition. So you spend a day looking at things that don't exist. The flyer advises you to wear sensible shoes and to bring your imagination.

The question is not 'what is there to see when there is nothing?' but whether the unbuilt city is non-existent any more if you are able to go for a walk in it. If we adapt the question to the wider world, are we supposed to judge humankind only by her recorded achievements and failures? Or would it be more fair to include her aspirations?

The fact that many of them are unrealised projects does not make human aspirations any less real, as long as we recognise them. If one were to organise an 'Unbuilt World Walk' through human history, it would require more than sensible shoes and simple imagination. For our eyes to see the human determination to create beauty, we would need compassion and moral conviction. Such a stance would be extremely helpful and supportive for today's human, for despite all her ostentatious cynicism, she desperately, yet secretly, still has faith. It is not easy for her to admit this. She is not so different to me, fighting with the word hope, resisting her need to believe.

A group of New Yorkers trying to erase swastikas from the tube windows one early morning; an illiterate old man who carries firewood to a children's library of his own making in a tiny Anatolian town; Lebanese protestors singing 'Baby Shark' in their thousands to send a baby who had been stuck in the traffic off to sleep; residents of Hong Kong taking their friends from the hands of heavily armed police; Chilean women standing up to police brutality through dance; Irish school kids organising to stop the deportation of their Nigerian friend. These are only a few moments from hundreds that people have shared on social media in recent years. We share them because we want to believe in the human, and to refresh our faith by witnessing its determination to create beauty. As if trying to cure the media of its obsession with the absurdities and tragedies that fill it, we share posts in which random people are doing the right thing. The popularity of such posts and the aching joy we feel when sharing such moments are only one piece of evidence of our eternal need and ability to believe in the human.

One might think that the hardest part of such faith is to have a formidable moral conviction, or to forgive people more than the pious forgive God. But among several other challenges the most difficult one actually occurs in a seemingly less significant place. You. Here's the biggest dare of all.

'*Sit autem puero huic incredibili conscious, sine fine amore et roboris habitat. Sit huic puero nisi obviam populo ...*'

I am standing in the middle of my Zagreb apartment reading in Latin from a piece of paper. Baby Valentino is in the centre of the room. He is held by his father Victor, who is Spanish, and his mother, my close friend Burcak, and they are both giggling. There, at the heart of our silly ritual, sits a serious commitment: I am becoming Valentino's secular godmother. And these are the words that bind us:

> May Valentino bring only joy, prosperity and good fortune wherever he goes. May he see the whole world and understand humanity better than his ancestors. Today, my child, with the permission of your mother and father, I become your secular godmother. Hereby I promise to be your protector, your guide and your companion for the rest of my life.

With a 'what the fuck!' expression on his face, nine-month-old Valentino cries towards the end of the ceremony, because of my scary churchy tones that imitate baptism scenes from the movies. And as cruel adults we laugh even harder at his sad frown.

But in truth, there is nothing to laugh about. Because it is tragic for us, people who want to believe in the human, to lack the structured, non-religious rituals that might seal our promises to one another. It is a serious business to promise a child that you will be present at all times; considering that I don't even feed the pigeons that come to my window, fearing that I might disappoint them one day, it is a huge leap for me. By making such a promise I not only have a responsibility to be present but I also have to have faith in myself to perform the job.

That, my friend, is the biggest dare I have set myself. Going into wars, risking death or other dangers in life is nothing next to the fear that derives from such a risk. The hardest, and the most divine – can I say that word? – part of having faith in the human is having to believe in oneself.

I am not sure whether the grey-haired woman in Edinburgh meant all these things when she told me to think about faith. But what I now understand is that it is useless to fight against the magical power of the human that only faith can generate. And hope is just a timid code word that implies this need for faith. Today's political movements, the ones that are determined to set a new direction for humankind or are proposing an exit from our political and moral maze, should not neglect the people's need for and ability to have faith. As explosive as the word faith may be it also sits at the very core of the question of political action. We should all come to terms with the fact that faith is and can be the only reason to act when all is lost.

Because believing gives us the ability to make promises and the determination to fulfil them – to create beauty, all sorts of it. My hand does not pat yours while you are reading the menu of Restaurant Hope. I seize the hope-menu from you and put my finger on your chest, saying, 'I believe in you. And you can believe in me. You must.'

2

Choose the whole reality

The cage is so small that the bear hardly fits inside it. He hits his head against the iron bars; fresh blood gleams and leaks through old brown scabs. His mouth is open wide in an inaudible roar. We stop to look at the bear together, me and the pelican. Dragging her broken wing, she has led me here. Now her beady eyes – the only signs of life in her mud-covered body – flit between her friend and me. There's no need to know the language of the beasts to hear the cry. 'Help!'

The Hilton Hotel was the safest place in Erbil, northern Iraq for journalists, spies and all the other regular visitors to war-torn lands. The fresh holes in its walls made by anti-tank missiles contrasted with the plastered-on grins of the heavily armed Kurdish militia standing at the sandbagged gate. A few days after the execution of Saddam Hussein, turbulence had once again returned to the region: Iraq was being reshaped through oil-soaked international negotiations.

Meanwhile, on the Hilton's roof terrace bar, the supra-national entrepreneurs – the only cheerful faces in such times – were making deals and drinking with sex workers smuggled across from Baghdad by a Turkmen pimp. The barrel-chested young man's crooked wig shifted as he played the Casio keyboard, providing the bar's musical entertainment, and especially when he was negotiating prices for the women. A 'redundant' girl was obsessively peeling off her nail polish in a dark corner, checking her hands each time the light from the mini disco ball hit them.

As ever, it was the best of times for the few, the worst of times for the rest, yet none were interested in the deserted zoo behind the hotel. Had I mentioned the two abandoned souls – the bear dying of madness and his stoic comrade the pelican – nobody would have believed that they were real. The moment we were living through was, once again, too crowded for true stories.

Reality is a vast land, and one that encompasses the realm of the magical. Indeed, magic germinates first and foremost in reality. On any given day we might see a determined poppy breaking through concrete, take our time to watch the unmatched might of a fragile newborn baby, or when walking along the street with hunched shoulders suddenly spot a piece of graffiti that answers all of our questions.

But when times are extraordinary or confusing – as they are today – it might sound naïve to say that reality is the true home of the magical. In such times, when the word 'real' becomes terrifying, evoking only the perfect shitstorm outside our window, many of us make a secret deal with life. We constantly try to calculate the optimum distance we should stay from reality: close enough not to be completely out of touch but far enough away not to be hurt. However, reality has a devious habit of vindictiveness; sooner or later it will take revenge on those who think they have successfully kept themselves safe and clean by smartly evading its dust and mud.

'No, no. It's too late. I can't forget who he really is, even when we're making love. It's maddening.'

One of my friends in Istanbul was in a reasonably comfortable and tolerably boring marriage, and like many such marriages it was supposed to last forever, until one day it didn't.

She had drawn up a substantial list of 'official' reasons for their break-up, which she would offer to curious relatives and the outer circle of her friends, but none of them had been the actual deal breaker. 'How could he … I mean, how could anyone not go down to the Square during those weeks? Not even once?'

she pondered. The secret reason behind her divorce, it turned out, was the Gezi protests.

In the summer of 2013, my country had rebelled. The heart of the protests that spanned the nation and all its political factions was Taksim Square's Gezi Park. And my friend's apartment happened to be a five-minute walk from that hotspot. Although she had been proudly apolitical until then, that did not stop her from going to Taksim, sometimes just to see what was going on, at other times to join the protest. History was in the making, and being outside of it was not an option for her.

Her husband, on the other hand, a hedge fund manager, found 'this whole charade' first childish, then dangerous and overall too off-limits for his conservative taste. The questions at the core of their break-up were not at all political; rather they were simpler, yet more crucial:

'How can he not at least be curious?'

'What am I going to do with this detached man for the rest of my life?'

'Are we going to lock ourselves away in a castle and watch life passing by our window?'

When trying to describe the feeling she had whenever he touched her, my friend couldn't decide between 'disgusted' and 'vicariously ashamed': 'I can't even kiss him any more, you see?'

That same year, several of my friends and acquaintances' marriages and relationships broke down for the same reason. Yet many new ones began. By 2014, those who didn't dare to touch reality found themselves no longer being kissed by those who could. And those who immersed themselves in the dust and mud of reality could not bear the tofu taste of those who chose to confine themselves to their castles.

Taking this tofu stance towards reality, however, is not an individual matter. In fact, ever since the late 1970s, when the business of fearing reality started to take off, most of us were already beginning to be shaped by it. And since then the economic system, empowered by the dominant culture and a conservative sense of morality, has kept imposing on us the idea that the world is an impossible mess we all have to protect ourselves from. By the eighties, the idea of building our own, untainted, individual realities, proportionate to our purchasing power, had turned from immoral to normal. The world's reality had begun to look like an incurable disease that only the poor and the unfortunate had to suffer. In order to stay healthy, we were supposed to work hard and buy up personal space and time, so that our individual realities would be completely free from the dirty burden of the world.

It has been so liberating, imagining ourselves exempt from the political and moral burden of having agency. And in this new setup, if injustice still made you feel uncomfortable, you could ease your conscience through small good deeds – like throwing a few coins to an online charity or sending out some positive energy. Or you could always hold hands and repeat the new wisdom of our age: to know the difference between the things we can and cannot change, and to accept the latter. While the dangerous beast of reality had seemed to be safely caged, it was in fact us humans who had been banned from entering its realm.

In return for being exiled from reality, we have been offered as hush money a never-ending childhood, a right to eternal carelessness. The adults would take care of the boring business of reality. As the Peter Pans of history, we may not have been the proudest of generations but we had the widest grins in history. We did not even remember forgetting the times when things were different. What previous generations lived through when they were less fearful of the world's reality had all been deleted from our memory.

'But then maybe it's impossible to erase that memory,' I said to Ali, in his apartment in Zamalek, Cairo. After a long day of talking to protestors on Tahrir Square, I was having dinner with my new Egyptian and Tunisian friends. For the last ten years, Ali and his wife Ranwa had been running Arab Digital Expression, a platform set up to educate young people about the digital sphere.

Many of the new prominent activists on the Square were actually their former students. We were supposed to be discussing the day's events, but then, while scanning through their library, I saw something surprisingly familiar.

'Ah, is this *The Little Black Fish* by Samed Behrengi? It's the first book my mom read to me.'

'My father was the first publisher of that book in Palestine,' said Ali in a broken voice. We recalled the story together: the Little Black Fish leaves home to discover the Big Sea. He runs into several creatures but ends up getting trapped in the pouch of a pelican. He meets many small fish there and organises them to fight together. They join forces and free themselves from the cruel pelican ... Our voices overlapped, 'because the small fish are strong when they are together.'

Thanks to the similar history of our lands, our shared laughter was tired: his father had been persecuted for publishing such books, and my mother had been imprisoned when fighting against the pelicans. It was an ironic twist of history that found us both now living through a resistance movement, like two adult Little Black Fish, and recalling the stories of the bloody 1970s when people like us from the previous generation had been killed, imprisoned, exiled and tortured all over the world for rejecting a system in which big fish eat small fish or the might of the pelicans makes them right. Here we were, coming from different countries, swimming together again to change reality. This was not magic but reality.

Eight years later in Brussels, I was reading *The Little Black Fish* as a bedtime story to nine-year-old Nova. The book was my birthday present to her. Funnily enough this was the first time I had actually read the book by myself. The story was as beautiful as I remembered and I was trying to imitate my mother's animated reading, especially the bit about the Little Black Fish organising the other small fish to beat the pelican.

But then, as I scanned the words before I read them, I came across some lines that I had never heard before: 'And then the Little Black Fish never came back home and nobody heard anything more of her.' A bitter laugh escaped me – probably a little terrifying for the kid – and I paused.

Nova, my little fish, was curious about the ending. 'Then? What happened then?'

So, I finished it. 'The Little Black Fish came back home and told of all the wonderful things she had seen in the big sea. All the fish were mesmerised.'

It seemed that, four decades ago, my mother had deceived me into believing that the story had a happy ending. It was quite an artful way to seal a child's destiny as a storyteller, to shape her as a person who chases the tail of reality in order to catch the magic. So I decided to imitate my mother, choosing to read the

ending she had made for me, in the hope that Nova
would herself grow up to become a small fish who
was not afraid of reality, and who would stand with
the right not the might. After all, it is rare that reality
passes the ball, allowing us to score a goal on behalf
of the magical and the beautiful. One has to strike like
Maradona – even with the hand of God – when one
can. And I am part of that reality, as Ali's father and my
mom were once. But even when reality doesn't offer us
the chance to score such an easy goal against the rule
of the cruel, there is still a chance to dribble the ball.
The ache induced by reality can only be eased in reality
itself. Even when that reality is not a bedtime story, but
a proper shitstorm.

The white parrot in the cage has a self-destructive
temperament. She is depluming her feathers – or what
is left of them – while grumbling in Arabic. The reason
is probably the place where she lives.

This unfortunate parrot happens to reside in Sur,
right on the Lebanese–Israeli border. It is the summer
of 2008, yet another turbulent time. She lives in the
Orange House, a small hostel owned by two brave
women. The hostel's front garden opens onto a beach
that stretches between two enemy countries, and both
armies collect the sand for their sandbags from here. It's
also where *Caretta caretta* turtles choose to lay eggs.
The two women are there to protect the eggs, especially

from the Lebanese soldiers who do their daily training in their front yard. This entire geopolitical burden is probably too much for the parrot, so she is going bald and cursing before our eyes. It's a tragicomic moment that makes laughing both irresistible and mortifying, so I purse my lips.

Apart from the parrot's fury, the place is silent – and silence is a luxury item in the Middle East. The small banana plantation between the Orange House and the beach is scorched by the sun. While looking at the bananas I remember something I was told the first time I visited Lebanon, in 2006, just after the Israeli attack on Beirut. An old woman had explained to me then that bananas make a sound when growing and that if it is quiet enough you can hear the banana plantations going *chouk chouk chouk*. I ask the owner if that is true.

'Oh yes,' she says, and imitates the sound. She pretends to be angry, and gestures at the balding bird. 'If this one stops cursing you might hear it yourself.'

Suddenly the parrot falls silent, but then, it begins mimicking the banana sounds.

'*Chouk chouk chouk ...*'

We crack up with laughter. Mine is light, hers is exhausted. With a sigh, she gets up to walk to the beach where she will have one of her routine quarrels with the Lebanese soldiers. As she approaches the beach her steps bounce. Her joy resembles happiness. But only by being close enough to the reality of her life can one know that it consists simply of being fully alive. Happiness is irrelevant here, yet the joy is as much a part of reality as the fury and the devastation.

How much do we lose when we choose not to witness such joy while trying to protect ourselves from being wounded by our times? Can we measure such a thing? I wouldn't know, because as a Beiruti friend, Ghassan, once put it, I am 'one of those mad people who runs towards the shit, not in the opposite direction like one should'. This annoying habit of mine also happens to be the obvious choice for a storyteller. So, that day, after leaving Orange House I started writing *Banana Sounds*, my first novel, in which I tried to imagine which sounds would be audible in the Middle East if the noise of war hadn't swallowed them all. I don't think I would have been able to imagine such stillness in such a land, had the woman in the Orange House not dared to silence an army single-handed just to protect a few eggs.

It was during my time in Beirut that I learned it is possible to end up missing war itself. Not the blood and the death, but the stark reality of it. More precisely, what one misses is the version of oneself that emerges, fully alive and bold, at such times. For even though we might like to keep it a secret, most of us do crave being part of a real story. Not because we want to be the most interesting person at cocktail parties but in order to make sense of life, to learn our true limits and to test our moral weight.

So perhaps our fear of reality, and the reason we make secret deals with ourselves to keep an optimum distance from it, is also, in part, the fear of seeing what our true selves might be like when inside that reality. We imagine that, were we tested properly, we might end up failing, morally as well as physically. It is this fear that leads us to scream 'enough' at our screens, before turning away and switching them off. The shame provoked by our indifference feels more manageable than the risk of being broken by an encounter with what's real.

But from this point on, our relationship with the world becomes merely the uneasy act of peeking out at it every now and then. In our haste to secure our own happiness and protect ourselves, we forget that we also need magic to see that life is not a realm of terror to be feared, and that magic only becomes visible when we are close enough to reality to touch it. It is distance that deepens our fear, and reality is always less terrifying than it seems from afar. The self that is revealed in the context of reality is always stronger than we had imagined it to be.

It is easy to forget these facts in a world that is full of opportunities not only to be the reluctant spectators of a pitiless reality, but also to be performers competing to upstage the 'reality' of others. Adopting this performative 'self' has become the new normal. It has happened so fast that parents who in their childhoods were taught to despise the wicked queen who was full of herself when saying 'Mirror, mirror on the wall ...' ended up with children who are not only constantly looking at their own faces, but also making a profit out of it. Four decades ago we would have felt pity if the men wearing adverts on sandwich boards had put on a forced smile, but today children faking happiness on their social media accounts seem quite ordinary.

This transformation has occurred neither through our conscious choices nor as a result of visible oppression. We have simply had to reshape our existence in order to survive in a world where every entity, from the state to the individual, has had to transform itself into a company, the only possible structure in society's current setup. Alas, anything that fails to operate like a company is destined to perish. Viewed through this lens, humanity seems irrefutably fake, selfish and profit-oriented: a collection of creatures who willingly perform not only in selfie videos but in every waking hour, even when they are not making money out of it. It has become quite difficult to remember the simple fact about humankind: its magical power and its beauty is only visible when you too are there, without the mirrors, and only when you are close enough to touch one another.

* * *

'Oh yes! We are blessed, really. Every night we dip our bread in the sea!'

Kiraz, a forty-year-old woman, is laughing. The other two women in the shack join her. This is Küçükarmutlu, a poor Istanbul neighbourhood at the top of a hill over-looking the Bosporus. Today is their 'collective crêpe suzette baking day', as Kiraz named it after learning the words 'crêpe suzette' at the home of the wealthy family she cleans for. 'Collective' on the other hand is a staple part of her vocabulary, as this hill has been a well-organised Leftist stronghold for decades. It's the only reason they hang on to their district, which has become too valuable a piece of land for the poor to be allowed to live on.

Today they are cooking pancakes for several families, for as long as the camping gas stove they all chipped in to buy lasts. I am sitting Indian-style on the sofa, which doubles as a bed for Kiraz's daughters, and asking them questions about poverty. At this moment, in 2007, the poor are being kicked out of the city to be piled up in ghettos. Like any other metropolis, Istanbul no longer needs cheap labour like she did in previous decades. I am going around the city talking to the poorest of the poor in order to document how they survive. And this is how Kiraz navigates the injustice of her reality.

'That evening, they kept me late so I missed the only bus coming here. The man of the house gave me a lift. The family was supposed to give me a raise. You know these people ...' she intuitively avoids me as a member of the middle class, instead turning to her own, to her friends, who also work as cleaners. 'Oh, they freak out when it's time for a raise. Beating around the bush etc.' Her eyes are back on me, expecting some under-standing. 'You know, they drive these cars, live in those places, they make us work without any social security and yet I am embarrassed to ask for a raise, but he is not ashamed to ... Anyway. The guy sees my shack and goes, "But you have a life here, ah? It is certainly better than mine. A house looking down on the Bosporus!" I don't know what came over me. The car was still moving but I opened the door. He freaked out. I said, "Oh don't I know it! We are blessed. We dip our bread in the Bosporus for dinner!" Fucking bastard!'

The other two, goggle-eyed, ask: 'Did you curse? Did you?!'

Kiraz laughs. 'Of course not.' They wave their arms in the air with mock disappointment. But then they smile, as if forgiving this crafty touch in her storytelling.

Suddenly Kiraz shouts, 'Go away, bitch!' The family cat is trying to steal the *crêpes suzette*. Kiraz laughs at the poor animal, who has had to turn *vegetarian* to survive – another word she picked up recently. She tears off a bit of pancake and throws it to the cat. 'Here you go. Poor bitch, she wants to be French like us!'

For those who have no choice but to step inside *actual* reality and struggle with it, their resistance creates something quite powerful. By choosing only to observe this struggle from afar, onlookers deprive themselves not only of the chance to learn the craft of endurance but also its joy-inducing magic. When we keep a safe distance from reality, we fail to understand that those inside it are fighting with everything they have. The uneasiness of the spectator, her feelings of guilt and helplessness, are simply irrelevant to them.

'Fuck it. I can't watch this anymore,' wrote Ayşegül to our WhatsApp group. Let it be recorded that as of 2020, behind every great woman is a female group chat. This was ours: a rock star, an actress, two lawyers, a café owner and me. A tiny tool to make our lives a bit more bearable and help us understand the world's reality together. In the last two years, one of us had given birth, another had buried a mother and every one of us had got back on her feet at least once – all broadcast live with nimble thumbs.

During the last week of February 2020, we were yet again paralysed with shame, shifting between clinging to our screens to follow the news and peeling ourselves off them to curse. After Turkey's military operation in Syria, the Syrian regime's Russian allies had responded by killing Turkish soldiers. Turkey's President Erdoğan, who had been Vladimir Putin's buddy only a few days earlier, demanded that the European Union and NATO support him. World War Three was about to begin and

Erdoğan, as usual, did the unthinkable. In order to pressure Europe into an alliance against Putin, he decided to use Syrian refugees. In the middle of the night, he opened Turkey's border with Greece to 'flood' Europe with refugees. This was madness of the first order. Groups of refugees in Turkey – many of whom weren't even from Syria – were woken up and put on coaches heading for the Greek border, to be left in the woods. Some were taken to the Aegean coast to be smuggled by human traffickers.

Human rights violations were broadcast live on air, as the Greek border police sprayed people with pepper gas, and babies were put on dinghies heading towards the Greek island of Lesvos. Some locals on Lesvos attacked the new arrivals. It looked like a mass social experiment. By compressing the biggest moral and political crisis of our times into this Mediterranean island, it was as if the world wanted to observe how savagery flourishes among human beings. Ayşegül, like millions that night, was feeling the guilt of the onlooker.

The next day she began giving free yoga lessons to Syrian refugee women in Ankara, Turkey's capital. None of us were so naïve as to believe that you can change the world with small good deeds or by singing mantras. But hers was the simple urge to be part of reality rather than suffering the shame of distancing oneself from it. Or to put it another way, it felt even more useless to suffer paralysing shame than to be teaching the 'downward dog' position to Syrian women who couldn't have cared less about yoga but needed to do something, anything that would make them feel like a normal human in order to bear their own reality.

Ayşegül told me that only after the lesson was she finally able to inhale and exhale properly. The will to touch reality and the human beings within it was as simple as the urge to breathe, and breathe together. She told me that in such times as these we shouldn't give in to hesitation; we should simply start doing something, anything. She was right. After all, one cannot hesitate when it comes to breathing. And one learns that breathing in difficult times is something that requires another person to help you do it properly.

In any environment where women are for sale, the relationship between a woman who is selling herself and one who is not, can be awkward. She thinks you will be condescending and you think she won't want to waste her time when she could be doing business; the roles you are given in a man's world get in the way. But then what are alcohol and interesting times for, if not for rising above such ill-fitting roles?

The girl in the darkest corner of the Hilton roof bar who has been peeling her nail polish hides her hands as I approach. I make small talk, trying to signal, 'I'm harmless.' When she finally forgets about how her hands look, I tell her about the bear and the pelican. *Oh no*, she *can't* believe it. And *oh no*, I *can't* believe that she is in fact a university student. As she talks about her wider, yet currently invisible, reality – the university, her friends and her dreams of continuing her studies abroad when enough money is made – the misery of our visible yet limited reality loses its gravity.

As our shoulders touch, her body seems to lift and become more substantial: stronger yet lighter too. She taps her finger on the whisky glass. Her giant fake emerald ring chimes faster than the Turkmen pimp's Casio organ. It seems to me that she is tapping out the rhythm of her larger reality, in which she will magically, yet certainly, thrive.

'So,' she asks in a surprisingly loud voice, 'where is this mad bear exactly?' The entire bar turns to look at us.

I raise my own voice in an act of solidarity. 'Not far,' I answer cheerfully. 'Actually quite near.'

As we laugh, I imagine we must look like two resisting comrades in a wretched human zoo. Our joy becomes visible only for those who are close enough to see, and who know that the cheer of breathing together can be part of even the worst kind of reality.

3

Choose to befriend fear

'Here, hold my hand,' I whisper to the middle-aged woman sitting next to me. Her Louis Vuitton-covered body abandons etiquette the second the plane is hit by turbulence. Her hands have clearly been searching for something more solid than the armrests, so I make things easier for her. It must already be apparent to her anyway: turbulence is my natural habitat.

Now she is grabbing my hand so firmly that, disregarding her age, I soothe her like a baby. 'I know. I know. It's OK.'

Her eyes are like a child's, begging for reassurance. 'Is it? How much longer until we land?'

By the time the plane makes its bumpy landing in Brussels, she is squeezing my entire left arm with both hands. But then in the few moments that we wait to get off the plane, her gratitude fast-forwards back to her stiff LV self. I turn my head away, making it easy for her to avoid me in comfort.

Finally, before she disappears at the double she snaps a thank you, which I hear as 'Damn you.' It must be the expression on her face. A first-class bitch flying economy, I think. My vanity at having been her rock for only ten minutes makes me forget that this is how fear actually works on people.

When we are hit by the blizzards of horror, our human response is no more sophisticated than that of chicks, squeezing their bodies together to shield themselves from danger. We instinctively offer a hand to those who are afraid, for we all know, viscerally, that only the reassurance of thirty-seven degrees of human warmth can dissolve the ossified spirit of someone who is terrified. But then, when the fear has passed and we eventually regather our wits, the first thing many of us do is walk away at the double from the version of ourselves that was revealed in that fearful moment, because suddenly it seems too feeble to be included in our internal selfie album. Delete!

It is the fear of *fear*. It is such a powerful driver that we do not even notice what we have lost when we erase fear from our recorded stories. For these are stories that also bear witness to the truth of our fragile selves, and to the profound beauty of real, spontaneous solidarity that arises between people in times of fear. By deleting these embarrassing moments we also erase the kindness and generosity offered to us. Had we less fear of *fear*, our photo album of the human would be complete. Just as seeing the empowering magic in reality requires us to be close enough to it, we need to choose to be intimate with fear to see how much humanness it actually includes. After all, considering the state of the world, we might all need such a close-up image of fear.

'I'm scared.'

My next-door neighbour in Zagreb is a giant of a man in his forties. Except for the scent of weed that leaks into my apartment every evening around 7 p.m., I have never felt his presence. And not once in four years had I seen him – until 23 March 2020, when a 5.3-magnitude earthquake shook Zagreb. It was only one week into the coronavirus pandemic lockdown and at around 5.30 a.m. I woke up to a horrible hoarse crackling coming from the depths of my apartment's concrete, as though a monster were being resurrected within the walls. Unhurried, I went through the checklist in my memory that has been there since the 7.6-magnitude Istanbul earthquake in 1999. Where was I supposed to stand? How do we do that 'life triangle' thing?

As my brain opened its memory files one after the other, I decided I couldn't operate without a coffee. While I was brewing it, the aftershock happened.

A second coffee, which I thought was absolutely necessary, coincided with the third shock. When the walls
finally stopped groaning I decided, with the total detach-
ment of a diplomatic observer, to check the staircase to
see if there was any damage to the frame of the building.
And that is when my giant neighbour showed his face.

Almost in tears, he opened his arms, muttering, 'I'm
scared.' With my coffee in one hand and a cigarette in
the other, I gave him a friendly, concise speech about
the different types of earthquakes, the soothing hori-
zontal lines of the cracks in our walls, and explained
why this earthquake was not so dangerous. As his face
muscles loosened, his voice broke when he asked, 'Can
I knock on your door if I'm scared again?'

Yet despite the numerous aftershocks that lasted for
several weeks, he never once knocked on my door. If
he had, he would have seen that I was prepared for
him, ready to offer soothing briefings about aftershocks
and the best coffee in Zagreb from my cheap coffee
machine. Alas, instead, since then I have had to confine
myself to feeling his presence – with its pleasant herbal
scent – every two hours, rather than only every evening.

I pictured him as a shrunken giant, sitting alone,
cursing his feeble self and the bloody earthquake – the
first in 140 years – that had coincided with the appearance of the coronavirus. And the reasons for him to
feel helpless and terrified kept on coming, for at the
same moment the earthquake struck, it started snow-

ing heavily, and then, a few days later, Zagreb found itself engulfed by a dust cloud that had come all the way from the Turkmenistan desert. Several times I had to fight the urge to knock on my neighbour's door to tell him, 'Hey, relax. This is the new normal. And we're only going to make it through once we get comfortable living with fear.'

We are living in an age of constant turbulence, and fear is no longer a transient moment that we have the luxury of erasing from our memories. The various global crises are multiplying in so many different ways that our responses to them are becoming contradictory. Earthquake: Get out! Coronavirus: Stay in! Fascism: Get together to stop them! Coronavirus: Stay away from other people! Our new normal feels like being on a plane that touches the ground after a long and turbulent flight only to take off again immediately, to repeat the same terrifying routine of uncertainty.

Understandably, one of the questions we hear most frequently is 'Will this ever end?' *This*, though, is now our reality, and it encompasses both properly epic fears – such as the predictable apocalypse, a third world war, or another pandemic – but also more ignoble concerns: terrifying tomatoes, genetically modified to such an extent they might soon bite us back, or a wrathful ex-lover creating a fake social media profile to mortify us for the rest of our days.

This merry-go-round of fear imbues our times with a particular zeitgeist: that our lives have coincided with the most damned period of history. On the other hand, this proliferation and variety of crises provide us with the means to master how we should act when in fear. Every fear offers us another piece of knowledge about ourselves – and about others – that we can record in our memories to refer to in future crises. These pieces form part of the jigsaw puzzle of humankind that we endlessly build in our minds. One question becomes important in such a jigsaw: what is the true measure of our selves and our fears in the wider scheme of the crisis?

'But seriously, what are you going to do with all this cheese now?'

The night of 14 November 1999 was freezing cold in Düzce, a small town close to Istanbul and the epicentre of the 7.6-magnitude earthquake. It is two days after the disaster that has wrecked the entire town and I am broadcasting live for CNN Turkey from the garden of a middle-aged couple. They are both wrapped in layers of blankets, warming their hands at the fire that burns in an old cheese bucket. And they are surrounded by buckets full of home-made cheese, the kind only Greeks and Turks make; the only thing rescued from the rubble of their demolished home.

Still in shock, they cannot answer any of my questions unless they are about this cheese. The five-minute live broadcast centering around cheese probably looks to the viewers like an avant-garde French movie, not least because seventeen thousand people are dead and two hundred and fifty thousand have been made homeless overnight.

As the anchorman signals to me to begin wrapping up the cheese nonsense, I feel the urge to try one more time to connect with the shell-shocked couple.

'But then, only hours after the earthquake, thousands of volunteers from several cities arrived in this town. These buckets of cheese were rescued by them – in addition to several children and adults who were brought back from the brink of death. Two thousand miners have also travelled over three hundred kilometres to get here, where they have been working for the last twenty-four hours without any sleep. They entered the town like knights of the underworld.'

I see the couple are finally nodding their heads. But the enthusiasm in their nods is not just approval. It is more that hearing the story they have lived through, told in someone else's words, has allowed them to look directly at the fear they have felt and understand the essence of what they have just experienced. And not just understand the experience, but understand something about themselves and their fellow survivors. Now each of them races to tell stories of the incredible solidarity they have witnessed over the last forty-eight hours. The expression on their faces changes, and all at once the nightmare of

51

the rubble behind them seems easier to bear. The man, looking into the fire, smiles a broken smile, as if suddenly seeing a shared humanity in the flames.

When we find ourselves in fearful situations, our ability to trust people and confidently assume that others will trust us depends on how we choose to record the memory of that fear. And for this memory to be recorded justly and humanely, our personal fear has to be knitted into the wider scheme of the crisis. Only by noticing others and their fears can we understand that the opposite of being afraid is not courage, but the ability to keep our eyes open to the larger reality. Putting your personal fear within a wider perspective is the only way to see its actual size and therefore to be able to manage it. Imaginary fears are harder to deal with, but when our fear has real substance, as it does in today's turbulent world, then the only cure for it is to trivialise it by placing it in a wider perspective. Only then can we remind each other of our shared feebleness, our laughable misery and the beautiful fragility that our existence is built upon. Once we do this, we can even celebrate these moments of fear, for within them all the superficial, transient accessories of life – our Louis Vuitton armour, if you will – are jettisoned, leaving us with only our all-too-human selves. But being able to see both fear and our fearful selves in such a light requires a certain understanding of what it is to be human.

*   *   *

'[Unlike the director's previous work] the film does not play fast and loose with Great Issues.'

When director Stanley Kramer's film *The Secret of Santa Vittoria* opened in New York in 1969, the *New York Times* published a short review which, at the end, recommended seeing another film that had opened on the same day. It was not the first time a critic has missed the point entirely.

The Secret of Santa Vittoria, one of my favourite films, contains a short sequence that illustrates one of humanity's few 'great issues'. Painted on a wall is a quote by Mussolini which reads 'It is better to live a day as a lion than 100 years as a sheep.' Beneath the quote, Bombolini, the mayor of Santa Vittoria, played by the spectacular Anthony Quinn, shares his perspective: 'It is better to live 100 years – *Italo Bombolini*'.

Here is the story in a nutshell: the Nazis invade the small Italian town of Santa Vittoria. They are after its wine. The frightened, and normally useless, mayor Bombolini determines to save the town's much celebrated produce, but since not a single person in the town takes him seriously, he is having a hard time. As a fearful atmosphere descends on Santa Vittoria, the people begin to split into two groups: those who resist and those who would surrender. But Bombolini has a bombastic idea. The whole town will carry the wine, bottle by bottle, in a human chain to a secret bunker.

From then on, Bombolini's job is to repeat to the Nazi commander the same words: 'There is no wine!' The villagers' job is simply to stick together and keep the secret. In the end, the sheep-like people of Santa Vittoria win and the lionhearted Nazis leave without the wine. And we the viewers are left with a deep understanding of humankind: when in solidarity sheep behaving like sheep can still survive!

Over the last three decades there has been no popular movie or novel that takes as its subject the collective victory of the sheep. If you scan the repertoire of popular artistic and cultural production on the topic of disaster and crisis you'll see that almost all of them follow the same storyline: an individual (most often a man, although recently there has been the odd woman) trying to protect his or her family or to save the world single-handed. And when things get really serious as they are today, you see an ensemble of Marvel superheroes, a small pack of lions, coming together to do the job. These are stories of the *lions*, and they do nothing but convince the sheep of their total incompetence by repeating that only the *übermensch* can save the world; the rest of the sheep can only be interested in survival. This is why *The Secret of Santa Vittoria* is a great film: it says the collective resistance of the sheep can prevail over the übermensch.

It is also a long way from that other popular narrative of our times – the dystopian free-for-all. In this version of the disaster story, as soon as fear takes over the sheep become more like hyenas and begin tearing each other apart. This cannibalistic representation of humankind has proved equally irresistible in popular culture, perhaps because the image of sheepish, feeble humans is harder to sell to the masses than the distorted – yet still popular – Nietzschean interpretation of humanity that once was tweaked to stand at the heart of fascism. But neither human nature nor nature itself is actually that cruel. And if we could look past the popular narratives we have overlaid onto our history, we would see that the first thing that happens in a moment of crisis is not sheep turning on other sheep. Instead it is sheep staring at each other in blank-eyed fear, asking 'What the hell are we going to do now?'

Now, thanks to the age of infinite fears we are currently living through, we have the opportunity to witness with our own eyes the *real* story: that humans do not actually respond to fear by completely losing it. Instead, we are, by nature, more prone to embrace our shared fears and celebrate our meek selves.

In March 2020, for the first time in a good few millennia, the world experienced spring without a human audience. Our deserted cities gave the impression that the planet was imposing a global lockout upon humanity. Except for the stray cats and city square pigeons, pissed off at not receiving prior warning, nature seemed in such a happy state that many began questioning whether our presence on earth was strictly necessary. Meanwhile, we were expected to experience the fear caused by the pandemic in an unheard-of manner: by doing nothing.

In the beginning it seemed easy enough. So much so, that when some French men and women revolted against the stay-home orders, their fellow citizens reprimanded them, saying, 'Your grandfathers were asked to go to war, so the least you can do is to stay at home.' Within a few weeks, however, doing nothing turned out to be a war of a different kind, one that brought with it many new fears. On social media, videos of people going crazy immediately became part of contemporary folklore, and homeschooling parents began seriously questioning their love for their children. China, where the pandemic first began, experienced an unprecedented wave of divorces on the day that quarantine was eased. One by one, the certainties we held onto were proving to be as absurd – and as useless – as those buckets of cheese I remembered from Düzce.

Within the space of a week we were obliged to learn not to touch our faces, not to touch other people's hands and to stay still when our anxiety was boiling over. Covid-19 made all of our tools for managing fear redundant, and required us to resist all the instinctive physical acts of soothing each other. This time the sheep were told not to stand together but two metres apart.

Hands offering help were covered in latex gloves and voices reaching for each other were breaking up across our screens. Suddenly we were driven by a new imperative: to find new ways to STAY in contact in a contactless world and to record fresh memories for the world's brand new fears.

By April, the world was beginning to look like a battleground between social Darwinists and those following the line of P.A. Kropotkin, who wrote *Mutual Aid: A factor of evolution* in 1902. Kropotkin, being a Russian anarchist communist, was actually a committed Darwinist, but he strongly criticised the social Darwinists who proposed the theory of natural selection and competition as an ideal for human societies. His famous book, based on his observations of nature, set out to prove that species not only compete but also reciprocate in order to survive.

Covid-19 revived a few 'haters' of Kropotkin's understanding of nature. They took to the streets in the US with placards reading 'Sacrifice the weak', while protesting the Corona-related lockdown. Unfortunately, some of them also happened to be running the world's most powerful nations. These descendants of Mussolini wanted only the so-called lions to survive.

However, in real life, and during this very real crisis, these ugly specimens of humanity were in the minority and quickly became nothing more than a laughing stock. The rest of us, the majority, were instead sharing sheepish ways to endure these difficult times: paying one another's grocery bills, sewing scrubs and masks and finding new methods to help healthcare workers, or simply easing each other's – and our own – fears with reassuring words. Overall, the dominant attitude was to trivialise our fear as an act of solidarity and to mock those who took a position of lionhearted denial. It was as if a worldwide network of neighbours were telling each other, 'We'll get through this.'

Of course, we were not all 'in it together'. Some of us bought an island from which to enjoy quarantine; others had to go to work while watching the Instagram posts of the rich and bored. As thousands of scientists worked frantically to save humanity, other people made plans to profit from a future vaccine. Yet even then, the dystopian narratives of chaos did not unfold as predicted. The exploited, understandably or not, chose not to attack the privileged. There was no looting, no acts of retribution. We the sheep were learning that turning on each other and fighting happens only when all other options have been exhausted. This is neither bad nor good, it just is. Our belief that humanity is, in essence, self-serving and evil – a belief that has driven the dominant morality for centuries – was rendered irrelevant, even absurd, by the pandemic.

Instead people almost reflexively formed themselves into small Santa Vittorian groupings and began a Bombolini-style human chain to protect their humanity, resisting the paralysing effect of fear. Because, unless they are pushed in the opposite direction by the propaganda of imaginary terrors, this is what people *actually* do in times of apocalyptic crisis – and it is perhaps the reason why lions are endangered and sheep are not.

Mika and I look like surgeons who are about to operate on two glasses of gin and tonic on the bench across from my apartment in Zagreb. We are fully equipped for a very brief Corona happy hour: latex gloves, little bottles of alcohol and masks. We are two months into these extreme self-isolation measures, which are of Mika's own making. No official quarantine has been declared in the city, yet it has taken a thermos filled with the best gin in town to be served in proper glasses alongside some snacks – all carefully disinfected – to convince her to come out of her apartment.

'What's wrong with you, woman?' I finally asked. 'Why are you acting so weird?' She had been politely avoiding my worried calls and messages for too long.

She complimented my gin and tonic with her famous frown and said, 'I'm not afraid of the virus or anything. I just cannot cope with this reality unless …' a much-needed puff from her cigarette calls for a mask-less face, 'unless I pretend that it's the Bosnian War all over again.'

While sipping her cocktail, for the first time in four years she told me the story of her time in the Bosnian refugee camp in Croatia. 'I didn't talk to anyone and I didn't drink coffee for months.' (For Mika, talking and drinking coffee is an art form ...)

'Like Rosa Luxemburg,' I said, and we smiled at the memory of our brilliant, long-gone sister whose self-imposed rules were stricter than the prison rules, so that she could control her own time.

'I wasn't prepared for this new world of fearful uncertainty,' said Mika.

When I told her that I was also afraid of the future she immediately protested. 'No, no! Don't think about the future. You should just keep going. This is something you learn in a war.' By the time we had finished our gin and tonics and sent each other a kiss from across the two-metre Corona distance we were back to our reasonably cheerful selves.

In times of fear, 'the future' might be the phrase that is most minimizing on our perspective. It either obliges us to find a reason to be optimistic or it drowns us in worst-case scenarios of pessimism. It pushes the mind to operate in an impoverished duality of positive and negative, stripping it of its infinite imaginative capabilities. It paints the unexpected – and sometimes unknown – colours of all our possible realities in only rose pink or ash grey. My rejection of the word 'future' is not because I am advocating any new-age nonsense of 'staying in the now', but rather because only by focusing on our present and accepting the fear that comes with it will we remain aware of the fact that what we are doing *now* is what will determine our future. Keeping going means not just surviving, but also surviving beautifully, by being able to see – and to remember – our entire story, fear and all. And this also sometimes means embracing the sweet insanity that enables us to cope at those times when reality seems unbearable.

By May even my own extreme survival skills were almost exhausted. The solitude that I had always felt at home with became overwhelming. Yet my self-discipline was still intact; one-hour daily walks to the city woods. One learns only in extreme solitude that going crazy is about a sneaky normalisation process; the new perception of the normal leaks into your head with a certain relief which is not so very different to the sensation we all remember from childhood when we peed in our beds. The threshold of normal is lowered so slowly that it feels, well, *normal*.

My new normal in those days was blowing the seeds off newly appearing dandelions. The idea somehow stuck in my head that if we didn't blow the dandelion seeds away this spring, they might not appear next year. Also, looking for dandelions and an isolated spot to do the job was taking my mind off my fears. Each time I performed my mission, I came to understand and embrace the fact that little drops of sweet insanity are the best precaution against the truly terrifying madness of fear. These moments are the evidence of our beautiful sheep-ness that can endure the worst turbulences. And they are the antidotes that will prevent us from pretending to be stupid lions.

4

Choose dignity over pride

One morning in 2020, a video went viral on social media showing two guys forcing a robot to perform manual labour. The poor robot had been lifting and carrying boxes peacefully and with futuristic efficiency, until the men began beating it with hockey sticks and folding chairs, all with the terrifying indifference of a scientific experiment.

A few days later it was revealed that the robot in the video wasn't real. It was a piece of computer-generated animation, and the video had been posted by American robotics company Boston Dynamics for publicity purposes. However, the variety of reactions to the video was in many ways far more interesting than any of Boston Dynamics' ground-breaking technology.

Some were jokingly concerned that the video would one day, once the machines had taken over, make for perfect propaganda material against humankind. But there were many, like me, who instantly began struggling with reflexive indignation when faced with this act of humiliation. We held on to our original emotional response, despite the fact that the victim was not even a real machine but a virtual one. The reaction of this influential minority was so strong that a few days later the company posted a new video in which, tired of its mistreatment, the animated robot takes its revenge on the brutal humans.

Who could have thought that we would one day crave catharsis through a humiliated machine? Yet enough people apparently did. Even though the videos were intended to be yet another piece of ephemeral entertainment on social media, the saga revealed a silent consensus: even in the current system, of which we no longer assume dignity to be a fundamental pillar, we still have the ability to become agitated when it is under obvious attack.

The following morning I tried to imagine an android with a sense of dignity. I wondered if he could evade indignation or joke about it as dexterously as we did. Would disregarding his programming be as easy for him as it is for us? And how did we become so flexible about the dignity that has been encrypted in us?

* * *

'I don't want to go to school.'

This is what the eight-year-old me keeps repeating. It is 1981, one year after the merciless military coup in Turkey. Almost all the progressive and Leftist teachers are either jobless or exiled to remote towns, so my generation is left with the regime's favourite type: those who have willingly or unwillingly made their peace with oppression.

I don't yet know this. But I know that my teacher has dyed blonde hair, long nails with red polish, and that she is too happy. When you grow up on the side of the oppressed, happiness in others becomes a sign of complicity.

Although she adores me, I have a problem with the way our teacher treats the poor kids. She orders them to sit at the back of the class, randomly punishes them by hitting their palms with a ruler or humiliates them for being dirty. I am supposed to sit at the front with the 'good ones'; close to the throne. But I decide I want to sit at the back.

I don't really know the reason why, but I know that I get anxious if I don't sit with those kids. I also give them tactical advice on how to avoid a beating, which they rarely care about. It is impossible to articulate, but there is an invigorating and empowering joy in being at the back. Years will pass before I learn that this is one of those middle-class moral conundrums, but at that moment I am a kid taking enormous pleasure in being with those I have been told to avoid.

Finally, one day, after properly scolding me, the teacher asks the question out loud: 'Why are you sitting with the losers?'

I remember the impossible lump in my throat, and how my lack of vocabulary translated itself into unstoppable crying.

So, after school, when I finally make it home, I tell the story to my mom. The following week I am in a new school where my new teacher looks more *like us*, and Mom tells me that lump in my throat is called 'dignity'.

'It hurts when you can't shout,' she says. I remember her silent indignation, her moving jaw line, solving the problem of this moment through retreat and not by shouting out her own lump, all thanks to the terrors of military rule.

Almost always, somewhere at the beginning of our lives, we are introduced to the word dignity through pain and anger. And as soon as we learn the name of this pain, a wondrous yet terrifying world opens up before us with new things to watch out for. This irreversible process not only deepens our being, but invites us to become members of a particular cohort of humanity that, throughout history, has sacrificed itself to protect our dignity. In fact, we only truly become human the day we learn the word. We only begin to occupy a space as big as a human should when we are no longer shrunken by indignity. Sometimes we learn the word after the pain but sometimes the pain follows the word.

'If you are born into a poor family with too many siblings you cannot afford to be proud: you'd starve.'

The kids of the village are attacking the food, which has been placed on a tablecloth on the floor. There is a table in the village hall but it is reserved for the guests from the city. The guests, members of a 'strictly non-political' women's organisation, are there to celebrate 8 March, Women's Day, in this remote village close to Mardin, a Kurdish and Assyrian city in southeast Turkey. The celebration is brief and absurd: the city folk are put in the schoolyard where they give speeches to one another about gender equality and women's rights, while an artist silently performs some contemporary art thing by hanging mirrors on the metal fences.

Outside the fence the local Kurdish women are watching, not understanding a word but sensing perfectly well that they are expected to be no more than mannequins in this hastily arranged spectacle. As soon as the ceremony ends they disappear in a polite silence, but their kids stay behind for the only benefit: bread and meat. The city folk who are supposed to sit at their table and eat, stand at a distance and watch the kids with *ahs* and *oohs* that sound like pity rather than endearment.

There is a moral comfort in journalism; it allows you not to choose sides, at least physically. So at the age of twenty-five, I am in the outer circle of the room, perplexed. Harbiye, who is my age and the only teacher in the village, is standing next to me. She was born here to a poor family, one of the many siblings she mentioned, studied in a western Turkish city and learned about the gaze of 'strictly non-political' middle-class Turks. Her voice is peppered with provocation: 'You wouldn't have been so disturbed if you knew hunger,' she says.

'I'm not disturbed by hunger,' I reply. 'And the kids don't need to be proud. The adults could treat them with a bit of dignity, though.'

She is one of those Kurdish women with a formidably upright posture and tough facial expression: a feature implying that her indignation has been mounting through the years due to having experienced such gracious moments. But now, after my reply, I can see a trace of a smile at the corners of her mouth. She chooses her words carefully so as not to sound as if she is compromising: 'It is already too late for the ladies, but our children will learn very soon.' She still refuses to look at me. 'I will teach them that the bread poisons them if it comes with indignity.' Her jaw works non-stop as if she is trying to swallow something.

*   *   *

Although humankind quite recently decided to treat dignity as one of our intrinsic features, that might not really be the case. After spending thousands of years on this planet with each other, around the Age of Enlightenment we made a pact with the future, declaring that dignity would be our inalienable value. When Europe decided to rid itself of its monarchs, the powerless came together to make the privileged bow before this big word. After all the blood that had been spilt in the name of dignity, we decided that protecting this feature of humanity was worth the pain. Since then we have continued to teach the newest members of our kind about dignity, while we are still learning about it ourselves. And as we learn, we are changing both the meaning of the word itself and the process by which we learn about it. So much so that today we may be shouting out the word in a different way to those who came before us.

During the first decade of the twenty-first century people around the world filled city squares demanding the same thing: dignity. From the Seattle protests in 1999, to the Arab uprisings, to the large-scale protests in Europe and the US, millions of people shared the same cry as if tearing from their throats a lump that they had been trying to swallow for decades. These protestors were not pursuing their own material survival in a brutal economic system, or crying out for much-needed equality in a severely unjust world. In different languages, yet as if with one voice, they articulated that the value of humankind cannot and must not be translated into a market price. They demanded to be recognised as human beings and to be treated accordingly, with dignity.

These protests and uprisings were either suppressed or dismissed by the world's powerful. Then, a decade after Tahrir, something seemingly unrelated happened. The rising right-wing populist politicians who had begun seizing political power all around the world chose the word pride as their shared motto. In different languages they were organised and mobilised under the same banner: 'We want our pride back.' It was easy for right-wing populist politics to energise anger through this poisonous word, and versions of the slogan caught on: *For us, Hungary is first! Make America great again! Let's take back control!*

Amidst this noise it became more difficult to notice the immense difference between the two words – pride and dignity.

They seem close enough in meaning to be mistaken for one another. However, there is a crucial difference: pride divides the masses into 'us and them', while dignity is about an 'us' that excludes no one. This oneness is innate in the meaning of dignity. Dignity is about self-worth that requires no outer evaluation, while pride is related to the value that others grant to us. Restoring pride asks for *their* recognition through a violent act, promising that such an act will ease the pain of *our* broken pride. Demanding dignity, however, requires a total overhaul of the system that inflicts injustice, where only those who can afford it are treated as human.

Since the word pride took over the global political stage, those on the side of dignity have been fighting battles on two fronts: against the system that replaced human beings' intrinsic worth with a market price, and against those who, knowingly or unknowingly, spend their political energy in service of that same system. It is not a pleasant job to explain to people who are furiously looking for a sense of pride that they are, in fact, hurting inside, and that the hurt is called dignity. Correcting such a massive mistake is much harder than teaching a kid not to eat the bread of indignity when starving.

Thankfully, one learns dignity not only through pain, but also through the joy of defending it. And that was what all those people who filled the squares at the beginning of the twenty-first century wanted to convey to the rest of the world, not only through their slogans and placards, but by creating glimpses of a new life that becomes joyful only when you are on the side of dignity for all.

I have heard many people over the last decade express their disappointment in these protests, for they have not changed the world. However, what they did achieve changed history in the deepest sense: they began rewriting the story of dignity in a way that would transform the movements of resistance for the rest of our century. On a massive scale, they physically showed us the invigorating joy of sitting at the back with the 'losers' and performed the fulfilling lightness of saying no to the bread of indignity. They performed the most challenging act in the history of resistance: they built, in the city squares at the heart of their countries, miniature lives which showed what life would be like if they were to prevail over the system of indignity. And they performed the joy of this new life even amid tear gas and police violence. Coming from a range of different social classes, they also showed us that everyone could help to build the world and that nobody is too powerless to act like a person with dignity. All those people from different countries proved to us that the lump in the throat can be replaced with the cheer of having swallowed a cloud. They showed us dignity in its most delicate form, which is something we tend to dismiss.

On 26 May 2018 the French were applauding a young Malian man called Mamoudou Gassama. They had named him 'Spiderman of the 18th Arrondissement'.

A four-year-old was dangling from a four-storey balcony, and without a second thought Gassama scaled the building and saved the child. A few days later, French President Emmanuel Macron granted him citizenship, a medal and a job in the Paris fire brigade. Every news story about him said the same thing: Gassama had been in France for months as an illegal immigrant with no prospects at all until he performed that heroic act.

Even though my French is extremely limited, I watched all his interviews in Zagreb, where – after an emotionally exhausting process – I had been granted my temporary residency permit for the second time after having to leave Turkey for political reasons. Gassama's face was like a story constantly editing itself. The message he wanted to convey was that his actions should be considered not as a heroic, but as a kind, yet entirely normal, humane intervention. He chose his words carefully, trying to convince the world that he was not a wondrous victim but simply a human being. Because as Gassama and I know very well, if you take refuge in a foreign land the most curious deprivation that comes with your new life is that nobody asks for your help anymore. It is mentally and emotionally more manageable for the natives to see the refugee or the exile as only the receiver of help.

Welcoming a refugee with basic needs is always more manageable for the hosting society than accepting the fact that they might be welcoming into their space a real person, a new life. The temporary fulfilment of that individual's basic needs is less terrifying than imagining the refugee as a new and permanent member of their society. But then, being perceived as such is a strange form of loneliness that scores a fine line in a person. As the victim, who is only to be helped, your dignity is damaged in a way that is hard to describe. You learn that there are infinite ways of not recognising a person's worth as well as numerous ways of recognising it.

'We want to help. And we have a plan.'

It is the winter of 2009 and I am in a warehouse in Istanbul where a group of garbage collectors store discarded plastic and paper to sell on later. This is one of the city's most troublesome districts, Tarlabaşı. Although it is only a few hundred metres from Taksim, the heart of Istanbul, the district functioned – until the recent merciless urban plan was put into operation – as the home of the underclass and of undocumented migrants of all nationalities. Tonight I am having a meeting with the garbage collectors about my upcoming novel.

'Sister, as you know we owe you.'

I politely reject the idea. The so-called debt comes from years ago when I wrote about them several times in my newspaper column. Big capital, with the help of the municipal authorities, was attacking them. They were to be wiped from the map in order to monopolise the recycling business. At the time it meant thousands of families would be left without any income. So the garbage collectors organised in several cities to resist, and my columns might have helped a tiny bit.

Since several among them were book lovers, they were aware that night that my new novel was being published soon. So out of their graceful kindness they offered help. I politely accepted their secret publicity plan, not expecting anything really. To my utter surprise, within a few days many walls in several big cities had been stencilled with the name of my novel. I still think that it may have been the coolest book publicity operation ever executed, though until now I couldn't talk about it in order to keep our secret safe.

A month later I was once again in the warehouse to thank them. To be partners in crime had a sweet taste, but the more beautiful part of the evening was their joy when telling me the stories of their stencil adventure, all delivered with a knightly dignity and a hint of self-mocking. 'It was the fastest I've ever run from the police. Ha!' 'Remember the old woman who thought we were writing political slogans? My god, she was furious! "Literature, ma'am, li-te-ra-tuuure! We're serving civilisation here!" I shouted back to her. Ha! I got high because of the paint, we should do this again!' They seemed invigorated by being seen for what they really were: human beings able to help those seemingly in a better place than them. The joy surpassed the inequality that has placed us in different social classes.

*   *   *

Whenever we mention a human feature, such as love or dignity, which might have the power to cut through class differences and social inequality, there is always the danger of being misunderstood. Such claims require extra refinement. It must be made clear that dignity cannot be mended when there is inequality, and love is not possible when cruelty is the rule by which the system operates. But the problem of dignity goes beyond inequality, exploitation or oppression. Even if one lives a life with all possible privileges, one might still have to swallow the indignation of being dismissed as unworthy.

When the weather is balmy in the first weeks of spring, the Bosporus looks like a five-year-old's drawing of a spotless world. The sea is blue, the clouds are white and the sun smiles. In 2011 this picture fills the wide windows of my office at the newspaper. It is a big, fancy room, which I have filled with things that shouldn't be there: masks of Osama Bin Laden, Saddam and Gaddafi from Beirut; Hezbollah flags from Congo; trinkets from Armenia; gifts from political prisoners. Messy as it may be, my room is the only place in the building where liquor from all over the world is served; including silky cognac from Yerevan, the best – a small amount of – money can buy. It is another exhausted early evening after the newspaper has been sent to print, and the number two at the media holding suddenly stops by my office. He is a man of impeccable manners, so it is quite uncharacteristic of him to collapse his huge body into my armchair without a word. His soliloquy begins with a sigh of despair:

'The other day something happened. This is between you and me.' (Listening to the powerless is good, but to the powerful?) 'We were about to cut a big deal with a business owner up on the top floor with the boss.' (Nothing good comes from being a confidant to the powerful!) 'The TV was on and we were about to shake hands. Just then, the news shows this piece about the Kurdish question and, as you know, I'm a Kurd.' His face loses all its power-related majesty. 'He said, "We have to fuck them all and that'd be the end of it."'

He looked at me with the eyes of a wounded dog. 'And I couldn't say anything.'

Our paralysed silence was broken by the entry of the tea-man, a young Kurd who did not talk much. In a forced Istanbulite accent, he asked the boss if he wanted anything. Suddenly the boss switched to Kurdish, which for a second puzzled the tea-man. Hearing Kurdish in this building surprised him so much that he couldn't remember the words in his mother tongue. They exchanged only a few sentences but it was enough to transform their faces into a five-year-old's drawing of happy men. It was a quick fix of dignity for both sides.

Dignity is a word that has the capacity to cut through all the floors of society, from the very top where the big deals are done to the very bottom where the tea-man sits with drooping shoulders. That is why in today's world, in which our system is in its last act, the word might have the power to gather people to build a better life.

While I was writing these words in the first week of 2020, many Turkish social media posts read 'Remembering the best days of our lives'.

Although all the photos were filled with tear gas, those who joined the Gezi protests that swept the country for more than a month chose instead to remember the breaths of joy they took. Around the same time, on the other side of the Atlantic, in Minneapolis, George Floyd was shouting his last words: 'I can't breathe.' As his cry resonated with the hundreds of thousands who took to the streets in the US, Gezi veterans began to note the numerous similarities between the rebellions. They were pointing out the almost identical actions not as part of a serious political analysis, but rather from familiarity with people who, years later, looked just like them: joyous with their activated dignity. As solidarity demonstrations took off in European cities, it was as if a long walk was resuming after an eight-year hiatus. Halting though it may have been, the walk that once passed through Gezi Park – and, before that, through Cairo's Tahrir Square – seemed to have enough momentum to keep going from Minneapolis to Trafalgar Square, to shouts of the same word: dignity.

Today, one does not need to be a novice Marxist 'seeking signs of revolution' or an overexcited activist to acknowledge that Capitalism as we know it is in its last act. More and more people are openly shouting the fact: the contract of Capitalism violates not only the contract of democracy, but also the contract of human rights in which human dignity was once declared to be inviolable. And the peoples of the world are deeply hurt. It is not only the ache of starvation or the despair of helplessly watching this inequality or injustice; people are wounded in a deeper sense. And during the days I write about this core pain, all around the world we are watching what people can do. Once they begin feeling the joy of dignity they remind our kind that we are still learning about the word. And if we are reminded of the joy of dignity often enough, who knows – it might even be the word that changes the world. In fact, I'd bet on it.

5

Choose attention over anger

'See the big guy? He'll be knocked out soon.'

Like everyone else on the street, I stop to watch an early morning traffic fight; one of those classic Istanbul spectacles, popping off here and there randomly as if operating as pressure relief valves for the whole city.

The onlookers are relatively relaxed because we all know the routine: a few fists for starters, then grumbling from the audience about the loss of manners in today's world; and then, without any dramatic finale, within five minutes everybody is on their way, going about their business. And yet, even though we know how it goes, it is impossible to skip the city's unique accompaniment to every street fight: the minute-by-minute commentary. The morning commuters cluster in small, loose groups to carry out their instant deliberations. The middle-aged homeless guy standing next to me is anxious to share his educated guess about the outcome. He's as eager as a constantly failing kid who just this once actually knows the answer to the teacher's question.

'The big guy with the fancy SUV – he's the one who fucked up, you see – he'll soon be back in his car, defeated. Watch, he'll curse his guts out just to save face.' I turn to him for further analysis, and he manages to feign reluctance only for a second. 'In the end it's the angry, not the mighty, who win.'

Instantly my interlocutor becomes a better spectacle than the fist fight. His chest muscles are twitching with phantom punches while his eyes anticipate a victory that seems almost his own. He is suddenly alive in his weary body.

Such a sweet thing is anger. A deliciously sharp state of mind that cuts through the jungle of tedious complications. Magically blurring everything else, anger leaves you with the purity of a single emotion. Oh, how voluptuous is its simplicity. We all secretly love anger, for it is the only one of our emotions capable of cancelling out the power imbalances that render us weak. Believing that we all have this secret weapon makes even the meekest of us feel like a sleeping David, even – especially – when Goliath beats us on a daily basis. It is not a coincidence that the oldest story of all, the *Iliad*, begins with the word 'rage'; the defeated, the broken and the underdog become audible in history only when they are angry. Since time immemorial, rage has been the ink with which the written-off can write themselves back into the story of humanity. Therefore, we not only love anger, but we have also believed in its power since the day we began asking for justice.

Though, if I am honest, I am not sure anymore whether the anger of our times is sufficient to cut through the forests of complexity, to drain the swamp of complacency, to give us the just fight and finally the victory of the good, of the right. Can the little guy, with enough anger, punch his Goliath back into the SUV, or should the homeless guy no longer trust the wisdom embedded in his guts?

'So let's say you're angry at the flat-earther. Very well. How do you convince him? You show him a satellite photo of our planet. But he replies confidently, "Oh, that's Photoshopped." So you tell him that you went into space with several friends and saw with your own eyes that the Earth is round. He smirks, "We know who you are. You're a shill, you're one of those fake news guys." Now you're really angry. You spend all of your money to rent a spaceship and take the guy to space, let him see for himself that the Earth is indeed round. But with the spotless self-assurance of the ignorant he says, "Well, we believe otherwise."

'There you go; the problem has become a philosophical one. Now you have to prove that seeing is more valid than believing. Suddenly the assertion of a simple fact becomes a clash between science and faith. Met with this undiluted stupidity you roll your eyes, but still you decide to refight a battle you thought had been won in the Middle Ages. And now the question becomes political, because you have to rally the majority against all these soldiers of idiocy. You need to organise, to build a sense of solidarity between you and the seemingly few sane people left on this round earth. And that my friend, requires much more than being angry at the flat-earther, climate-denier, Trump voter, Brexiteer or Modi supporter, misogynist, free-market devotee, etc.'

This is me in Dublin, at Maynooth University, talking to a student after giving the 2019 Dean's Lecture. He seems unsatisfied with the title of my lecture, 'Joy of Dignity Against the Evil of Banality – The philosophical clash between the fundamental values of humankind and the politically imposed malice of our times'. He wants something more … something about rage, you see? He articulates the word 'rage' in such a way it seems the word fails him; he needs a word more infuriated than fury. He is not alone, and I do remember feeling like him. I have felt *really angry*. So angry that someone failing to express anger would shake my soul with wrath. Now, he probably thinks I am one of those ivory tower damsels entitled to play with ideas while

84

savouring the luxury of *feeling fucking nothing*. As his body twitches with the phantom punches he's directing at me, I pay attention to his anger. A new world of politics is being shaped behind his rage.

Throughout history, each time a new weapon has been invented, the nature of the fight has been transformed, as has humankind. In today's world we have a whole new battleground, entirely different tools to fight with. And therefore, as the footsoldiers of this new fight, we find ourselves in a moment of transformation.

Social media is that new weapon, and like radio and TV once did, it is reshaping humanity, the soul of our times and our fight for fundamental human values. However, at this moment, our situation is akin to that of the people who held electromagnetism séances when we first learned how to control electricity, or the elderly people who greeted the newsreader when TV entered our homes for the first time. We are still trying to figure out how to morally, politically and even physically position ourselves in this new digital age, let alone regulate it.

The benign appearance of our new technological wonder does not make things any easier. Social media, with its self-proclaimed dedication to 'free speech', creates the illusion that we are all equals operating in a public sphere, like the Greek agora where democracy was first built. Yet the platform where today's politics and morals are shaped is in fact someone's private

property. So, when we are engaged in politics, expressing anger or calling people to rebel, we are doing it in
someone's garden, as it were, wrongly assuming that
the platform belongs to 'we the people'.

The only benefit we get from this infinite, digital
garden is the joy of being allowed to exist online and
exercise our already basic human right to communicate. What we give in return is our personal data,
drawn from every like, comment and follow, which is
sold as a commodity to the highest bidder. In order to
generate more revenue, the owners of the digital space
require more data, and so they design their platforms to
keep us endlessly engaged. The only way to ensure we
stay there is to constantly stir our emotions.

For these companies this has been made extremely
easy. Over the last few decades our politics has been
infantilised to cast emotions as the leading actors of
our lives and our social interactions. What you *like* or
hate is the question, not what you think or what you
know. What you *believe* is the answer, never mind what
the truth is. This is quite convenient for the owners
of digital gardens because expressing emotion is a
never-ending occupation. As in the argument with the
flat-earther, there is no end to a disagreement based
on faith and feeling: everything must be restated and
restated, and, when fact fails, even the logical resort to
frustrated emotion. And the profit wheel continues to
turn.

Among the emotions, anger is the most engaging and by far the most profitable. Anger is also the most effective way for individuals to stitch together disappointments and fears in confusing times such as these. It provides us with the optimistic assumption that the anger we unleash will turn the power balance upside down. However, this constant expression of anger, with its illusion of political or social engagement, actually makes us even more submissive.

Within every language, anger communities are beginning to form, invigorated from one day to the next by gnashing their teeth at each new evil act committed by those in power. These communities create their own lexicons and their own codes, raising the bar when it comes to the magnitude of their anger. Driven by the fear of being deemed inhumane, each individual tries to keep up with the new standard. If one of them falls silent the community gets suspicious: *Is he a coward now? Did he give up fighting? Does she feel fucking nothing?*

The anger which is supposed to be directed at the unjust act or the evil actor gradually turns back on to those involved, or not involved enough, with its expression. Soon, engagement with these communities, and the constant articulation of anger, diminishes one's entire connection to the political sphere until it consists solely of fury. The noise of anger leaves almost no space for the mind to think clearly or to pay attention to what really is happening behind the rage, to the incident that induced the anger in the first place. When excessive anger invades the communication sphere, one fails to realise that if it were truly capable of cancelling today's power imbalances, anger would not have been allowed in this profit-oriented, private digital garden at all.

'3–6 month delay' reads the risk assessment report. It's a classic story: a company, in this case Alamos of Canada, is producing gold using cyanide in one of the naturally and historically most beautiful places in northwest Turkey, on Mount Ida and in the Troy Valley. As soon as the project got underway in 2019 the people of the region began to protest. Within a short time they were joined by thousands of others for what became an Occupy-type action called the 'Water and Consciousness Watch'.

In the face of these protests the company was forced to stop the project. And for a while it seemed everything was fine, so everyone who had engaged in the righteous anger necessary to bring the project to a halt, moved on to the next target.

However, after only a few weeks, thanks to some good journalism, the risk assessment report was leaked. The report analysed the public reaction, considering it a small bump on the road that would last no longer than six months. So, all that anger, all the best expressions of it, had in fact been calculated, monetised and included as an item on the list of expenditures.

After learning about the report, the people of the region reorganised their protest to make it more sustainable. No songs and carnival anymore; instead they would consistently show up on site. Unceasing attention became an integral part of their lives, because they knew that today the fight for human values or for nature depended on how long you could keep your attention intact, not how angry you were or how loud you shouted. And they learned that persistent attention couldn't be itemised on a company risk assessment report quite as easily as inconsequential anger. They had no time and energy to waste on expressing their emotions, so they paid full attention to the moves of the powerful, for they wanted the land and their children to survive. Though I bet they missed being angry, oh so very angry.

'I miss being angry,' I told my therapist.

It was the first time in almost a year I had asked for a Skype session. His smile pixelated on the screen as I began describing my state of mind: 'I'm not sure if this is a psychological question or a philosophical one, but I've noticed that I have recently quit anger. It seems irrelevant when one is busy surviving, maybe.'

When one focuses on survival as I have had to after leaving my country, when one lives in an uninterrupted state of insecurity, the emotions freeze. One's entire being becomes bound up with the idea of keeping going with one's dignity intact, and that leaves no place for anger. When you are genuinely powerless, you learn that expressing anger is a luxury, for true lack of power is that smile you force your face to wear when you want to 'spit on their graves'. It's the rictus grin you hold as you knock politely on doors that in fact you want to slam. And that bloody Nietzsche quote becomes a disturbing joke: 'that which doesn't kill you' nevertheless slaughters you in infinite yet invisible ways.

After I presented my revised version of Nietzsche's aphorism, my therapist said, 'But then you have to survive. Right?'

I laughed as one does when crying is the more tiresome option. 'It's the most unfair twist of history,' I said. 'I quit anger when it's finally back in fashion, you see?' I told him about all the newly published, beautiful books about female anger, and about how women, especially young women, are beginning to own their anger as a political statement. This had also been the case for the generation of women before me, but had unluckily skipped mine. 'So now, I envy the angry.'

My therapist, as he often does, mimicked my smile so I could see how sad it looked. I went on to tell him about my encounter with the angry young man in Maynooth, and how embarrassing it felt to be taken as the one 'feeling fucking nothing'. Together we remembered earlier times when I'd expressed political anger, years ago in Turkey, shouting at the powerful on TV screens and in newspaper columns, while receiving the applause of audiences who felt I was the megaphone through which their own voices could be heard. How grand yet alienating it had felt when people once granted me the title 'the brave'.

It was around this time I realised that the public intellectual is the gladiator of our times, and especially so in the years since social media became the main arena for so-called public debate. One takes on such a role almost unknowingly, simply by speaking the truth, but soon it becomes obvious that the audience is less interested in the political act of speaking truth to power than in applauding the anger itself. 'The brave' tells them, 'Do something, get organised. Say something. *Do you feel fucking nothing?*' and they simply applaud the rage.

'The brave' becomes a talking doll with a pull string, ready to be wound up by the audience following every evil act committed by those in power. The crowd takes pleasure in the familiar phrases the doll speaks, the repetition, and the doll, rather than the targets of those phrases, becomes the central focus of the game. There is too much self there, too much *me*.

'So to wrap it up,' I said to my therapist, 'this is obviously both a political and a philosophical question. Quitting anger wasn't entirely driven by my own survival instincts, it was also a moral choice.' He gives the same proper-therapist laugh that he always does when I wrap up my own session. But he's even more amused when I give a teaser for a future session, 'But then we have to think about the morality of surviving, *n'est-ce pas?*'

After the session I carried the question of the self-imposed aspect of anger and the morality of survival with me. The question was still there when I travelled to Budapest a few weeks later.

'This is with cheese, this is with meat, this is with potato and this one is with spinach.'

The middle-aged Hungarian woman has repeated the same words in English to each potential customer at least ten times in the last five minutes, and she will be doing this until sunset. Each time someone approaches to ask her which pastry is filled with what she will keep her smile in order to sell some more, at a few pennies each. The aching tension from that forced smile will be released during the night and next morning it will ratchet up all over again. The woman is one of many vendors in one of the 'ruin bars' in Budapest.

The ruin bar is a concept developed in Hungary during the 1990s, which spread to other countries the Danube passes through. It dates back to the time of the Iron Curtain, when the simplest freedoms had to be exercised in secrecy. Locals would gather in deserted buildings to turn them into organic spaces of fun and solidarity. The entire concept is dipped in the gallows humour that has always kept people going during the darkest periods of history. One of the ruin bars was called 'World Travellers' Club': a bar that served people who could go nowhere. Years later, a couple of entrepreneurs turned these spaces into touristy marketplaces with indoor cafés and bars that locals now avoid. Once secret spots of political freedom, ruin bars today have security guards checking visitors, who in a minute will be uploading the picturesque vintage details to their social media accounts.

The walls of the space are graffitied with slogans dating back to the nineties, a time when hopes of a more dignified life were invigorated in Eastern Europe, turning a generation into revolutionaries. Every bit of the space is touched by joy as well as the pain of the regulars from three decades ago. The middle-aged woman who today sells the small pastries might have been a regular back then; now, when not repeating the petty line that life has doomed her with, she is posing for the tourists' pictures as the exotic local.

What if I implore her, 'Be angry about this life that has turned you from a subject of history into an extra in someone else's Instagram account'? I bet she would take me for the new kid in this world of layered cruelties. She would assume I had no idea what survival really entails. She would imagine that because I talked about emotions, the idea of keeping going even with her dignity crushed was irrelevant to me. I didn't have to wear her forced smile.

Millions of people, whether in sweatshops or in fancy offices, share that same smile. They too miss anger and at the same time find it irrelevant. Devoid of the luxury of making the moral choice to quit anger, they are obliged to keep on going with their full attention on survival. I am not sure they need anybody to remind them of the beauty of anger. What they need to hear is a real, viable way out.

When anger is widespread enough that it has become banal, the absence of it looks strange, almost otherworldly. When we are all pushed to turn ourselves into exhibitionists, the one who stays reserved is considered weird or even sick. And when the dominant culture requires us to tell our personal stories, the one who does not is deemed distant, asocial and cold.

This is a story of a twenty-first century saint; an environmental activist who in 2018 became a worldwide figure.

Greta Thunberg has been accused of all those things: of being strange and otherworldly, weird and sick, distant, asocial and cold. These 'character flaws' of hers were scrutinised so much that she was eventually forced to talk about her Asperger's syndrome, just so the curious were given a medical reason for her temperament. The people who seemed to be waiting anxiously for an emotional crack, a meltdown or a bout of uncontrolled laughter were relieved: actually, she had a disease.

Greta referred to Asperger's as her 'superpower', a force that made lying or performing crowd-pleasing acts impossible for her. In a post-truth world where nothing is solid enough to depend on, where everyone is immersed in their emotions, this talent – or restraint – of hers transformed her image: an untainted, clear-minded sixteen-year-old girl in a world of confused sinners.

Watch any video of hers and you will see celebrity-filled audiences looking on like Romans, with Greta as the twenty-first century St Catherine (or like the corrupt French court and Joan of Arc), her face radiating conviction and commitment. Unlike the rest of humanity, not concerned about being boring, she repeats the same thing in a monotone: if we don't start believing (in science) we will burn (not in hell but) with the fires of global warming. Everyone falls silent as this secular saint speaks, not only because she is telling the truth and using facts, but because she doesn't show anger even when she says she is furious. What she does instead is present the world with a different way of being: a state of ultimate and uninterrupted attention.

What she has, and what she asks her followers to have, is the sort of attention that rises above today's noisy carnival of emotions.

Although the content of her words has nothing to do with the divine, her spotless and righteous faith in truth and in people seems almost biblical in this age of the hyper-mundane. Her determined attention and the accompanying consistent action look like symptoms of a syndrome, since it reminds people how much they are contaminated by cynicism, excessive irony and inconsequential anger. They begin to remember what they don't remember forgetting: how people act and what they look like when they are committed. It's as if the world is rediscovering the taste of decisive attention, and the possibility of replacing anger with resistance against distraction.

This may be because we are all beginning to realise that this time things are serious enough to demand our attention.

It might benefit all of us to realise that systematically forcing the individual to misplace their attention is a hallmark of fascism. Its unending bizarre spectacles, and the reaction to each of those infinite absurdities, exhausts the individual, finally beating them into an irreversible daze. Maybe we need to understand that we are now all in a survival state and there is no room left for anger.

Only rightly placed attention can cancel out these distractions while enabling us to focus our gaze on the heart of the problem. This attention will allow us to see the main arteries of our predicament, identifying how they course through the body politic of our day-to-day lives. Only by directing our unblinking gaze at the workings of the political machine can we avoid being dazed by the mesmerising yet insignificant representations of it that we are offered every day. Attention can enable us to see clearly the questions of our age, weeding out the infuriating spectacles manufactured to keep us busy. Otherwise we are destined to become perpetual raging bulls, like me years ago and like the young man at Maynooth University. And as a matter of fact, it is only when our attention is intact that we can find the serenity of mind to look around and see those who are in need of genuine solidarity: those who are silently suffering behind their forced smiles.

The fact that Greta is a young woman may not be a coincidence. She belongs to an uncelebrated tradition in the history of moral philosophy that has been pioneered mostly by women. Attention as a central moral stance has been explored by brilliant female thinkers such as Simone Weil and Iris Murdoch. It is an idea that all of us know without knowing: that anger, despite its empowering deliciousness, has limits when thinking of the world and the self. I am fairly sure that neither Simone nor Iris feared looking like a mad woman; suppressing their anger did not come from a desire to maintain an image of control. But they may have known that once anger encompasses our existence it leaves less space for the fragile, and therefore for the beautiful.

*   *   *

As the onlookers predicted, the fight on the street in Istanbul lasts only a few minutes. And my interlocutor's prediction proves right. The small guy with the wreck of a car throws the decisive punch. The heavyweight, half of his body already in the SUV, curses to save face. Before our eyes Goliath crumbles into pieces with embarrassment and David's lousy car all of a sudden looks rather more like a Mustang. My fallen king pokes me in the arm with his elbow. 'You see that? I told you. It's always the angry one. Do you have a cigarette, luv?'

He lights up, taking a long drag as if he were sealing his own victory. Staring at the empty space, he savours the moment. His eyes are moist. How we crave these moments of victory for our inner Davids, I think, and no wonder, when too many of us believe that it is only anger that will give us a just result. After all, it is all that we have in plenty and that the Goliaths have less of than we do. But if we manage to replace anger with attention, our victories might last longer than a few delicious puffs.

6

Choose strength over power

More than twenty years ago, in a remote village in southeast Turkey afflicted by a permanent water shortage, some 1,500 men gathered around an Olympic-sized swimming pool in a magnificent mansion for a peace meeting between two feudal lords. These talks would put an end to a long-standing vendetta. Carpets were laid out for the men to sit cross-legged and drink endless amounts of Arabic coffee, *mırra*, during the negotiations – and, later, to enjoy kebabs when the pact was sealed. I was twenty-four and the only woman in attendance. Like any rookie with aspirations to brilliance, I was certain that finding and interviewing one of the feudal mafia lords, a man central to Turkey's illegal state apparatus, was a great idea, especially when I was accompanied by a blond male photojournalist who looked even less masculine than I did.

As I stood in my jeans outside the mansion's enormous front door, building up the courage to enter, I remember thinking, 'Now, either I walk like a warrior queen or I vanish.'

My deep frown, the extremely long silk scarf that flapped as I moved and my exaggerated stomping worked: after ten minutes the middle-aged *mırra*-guy began acting as my personal servant, following me everywhere, and the men had begun addressing me as 'madam'. When you walk like you are somebody and keep your mouth shut, I learned, people tend to believe that you actually are somebody; a powerful somebody at that.

'But you can't walk like that – as if you're going to war.'

While writing *How To Lose a Country*, analysing the proliferating variety of political and moral evils that afflict the current moment, all while entirely alone in my Zagreb apartment, I decided that, since I couldn't do much about the damage in my head, I should try and at least restore my body. So began my pilates sessions with Asja, the most trusted personal trainer in the city.

The minute I entered the studio she was already fixing me. 'Darling, if you hit your heels that hard, your joints will be battered. Carry yourself, resist gravity. Be light. Light is strong.' Asja, being a former weightlifter, knows one or two things about how to resist gravity. Now in her fifties, her graceful moves assemble her accentuated muscles so that she approaches like a figurehead on the prow of a ship, magically rendering every wind friendly. Her soft tone gently leads your body to a place where you no longer fear the impact of buried stone as you fall back on snow. Instead you surrender, like I did, and begin to tell of your wounds and the stories of how you acquired them. I still remember the way Asja played along with my tough-cookie act as I told her how I invented my warrior queen walk more than twenty years ago.

However, Asja wasn't impressed at all.

Assuming she hadn't understood what I'd meant, I reiterated the basic gist for her. 'This is my way of throwing my weight around, you see what I mean?'

She smirked, 'Warrior queens don't walk like elephants, darling. There is a big difference between looking powerful and being strong. And I am going to make you stronger.' She made it clear from day one that our priority was to fortify my spine, to correct my posture so that I could resist gravity, not through some forced performance of power, but through true strength. 'Strength is invisible,' said Asja, 'it is not puffed-up muscles.'

The first thing she did was to put me in front of a mirror to see how twisted, crooked and contorted my body was. For the last four years, her mirror, or rather

101

my image in it, has been an integral part of our sessions. What I see there is a female body, an accumulated and complicated entity, still trying to figure out its true size and real weight in the second decade of the twenty-first century.

There is still no mirror in existence that can show the true size of a female body. Our bodies are considered both small enough to neglect and too complicated to comprehend. When in need of proper recognition they are considered too weak, and when craving a full embrace they are rejected for being too large. This is the female body: irreparably sculpted by three thousand years; burned alive when unwanted or, when burning inside with passion quickly extinguished; concealed or exhibited, squeezed and fattened, loved from a distance and monitored closely. Our flesh must be battered to be glorified, and is only celebrated when it is utterly vanished.

That omnipresent gaze, even when we try to forget or reject it, continues to tailor us to the liking of this or that power. Both the chin-up sulk of 'Fuck you' and the chin-down smile of 'Love me' misshapes our postures equally. And, ironically, both of these stances induce the same ache in the spine.

There has not been a day off for this body in centuries: for as long as we can remember we have either been resisting or submitting. Yet, whether light-footed as a ballerina or with the loud tramp of a novice warrior queen, we have still managed to walk this far. This bruised wonder, alas, is still the only address at which we receive life and respond to it. And here we are, standing in front of a mirror that is now filling with a rush of violent images, threatening to lay waste entirely the female body that is staring back. No woman is detached from this dark reality unless she rejects outright the idea of ever trying to find herself in the mirror of our times.

'I am so fed up with having to slow down when walking behind a woman at night so that she's not spooked,' said a male friend of mine from Turkey in 2019. The other men in the group began complaining exuberantly about how they too had had enough of being viewed as potential predators in this world of MeToo. The women in the group fell silent, eyes wide, speechless. 'Where to begin?' each one us was thinking. The fact that 474 women had been murdered in Turkey so far that year, maybe? Or that the majority of the men who committed 'femicide' were released because they 'expressed regret' in the courtrooms? Or with the inescapable conclusion that the ultimate reason for men to kill women would seem to be simply because they *can*? Yet here we were, my closest male friends working themselves up into such a state of affronted agitation that I found myself hesitating to say that, actually, it is a bit more difficult to be the woman walking ahead at night and constantly thinking that you might be attacked.

It is too easy to choose to believe that all the violence against women and the constant underestimation of it is happening elsewhere, among the 'yokels'. In reality, as I realised that day among my friends, the violence is everywhere and it actually begins the moment we say, 'Well, let's change the subject then.'

A global, salivating hatred against the female has been unleashed and this malice is not accidental. The attacks are sly yet devastating, intermittent but decisive. They come through an insignificant change in legislation or an easy-to-miss increase in a certain kind of man's confidence on the street. It is eel-like, slipping by us here and there. Its first impact is so slight that we either hesitate or are not alarmed enough to respond. And at times these attacks seem so absurdly outdated that many of us find them worthy of mockery. We change the subject, until we cannot. For, although our responses might be delayed, it does not alter the fact: a war is underway. Not only the female body and mind, but also what is female in the male, must prepare to engage. This war is not only against women. It is against all that is female.

However, something unusual, a beam of light, is cutting through the dark images in the mirror. As I write these words, Polish women are taking to the streets to protect their right to abortion. A few weeks ago it was the Belarusians who stood up in the squares of Minsk against a male dictator. At the same time, black American women were rising up against white male supremacy in a movement that inspired the entire world. In fact, the images have been piling up for a couple of years now: Irish women flying in from around the globe to vote against the ban on abortion; teenage Kurdish girls fighting the ugliest war of mankind all alone in Syria; Chilean women creating a global anti-rape anthem; Sudanese women chanting 'A woman's place is not the home. A woman's place is *al-thawra* (revolution)'; Indian women leading the most long-lasting protests against the ruthless leader Modi; Lebanese women kicking soldiers on the streets, demanding a just system; Iraqi women trying to make the long-neglected voice of a war-torn country heard.

As these images of darkness and light collide, the twenty-first century already looks like a worldwide war zone on the eve of the final, decisive battle. And this is what I see when I look at my body in the mirror: the battle scars of a warrior, one of the many warriors giving themselves over to this fight. Because in this battle, nothing female, not one single body, can afford to stand alone.

Three years after she began fixing the way I held myself, Asja smiled when I said, 'There might actually be a war coming. We might have to learn to be warrior queens.' She too must have seen what I had seen in the mirror. 'Well, in that case, we'd best be ready for the war,' she laughed, half-heartedly. Then she resumed her instructor's tone: 'Ready means active stillness. Align your entire body. Feel all the connections.'

All around the world the representatives of the Radical-male have been activated and are more emboldened than ever. The Radical-male encompasses the worst aspects of the human: destructive in its idiocy, calculating in its ignorance, self-righteous in its wanting. The Radical-male includes a wide spectrum arising from the dark matter at the heart of masculinity, and encompassing all that sterilises life, including the obedient in their feminine counterparts. Its ancestors are those who burned women alive whenever the power structure was threatened by chaos and igniting the fire to cleanse the world of complication was deemed necessary.

Today it is being organised and mobilised by the wide grin of the new fascism and is spreading across the globe. It is everywhere. If the act will consolidate their power, its leaders – whether in Moscow, Washington or Ankara – utilise the extreme piety of religious conservatism to inflame hatred against women, regardless of their religion. The capitals are falling one by one into hands more used to groping female bodies. The only way that the Radical-male can interact with the world around it is through wanting and seizing yet more power. But in that lies its weakness. The Radical-male is not at all strong, only an over-inflated act of power. It is, alas, armed with the state apparatus of some of the world's most powerful nations.

But these weapons are not only aimed at women. All that is female finds itself under attack. Female is also a wide spectrum, arising in the joyful matter at the core of a woman's body, and spanning all that is fertile to include the part of male identity that so many men have been ridiculed for embracing. The Radical-male cannot abide anything fluid, whether it is gender or rivers; everything has to be fixed for him to feel secure. All irregularities have to be made uniform. What is threatening both women's bodies and the earth is the same Radical-male motto: power means breaking; ruling means controlling; existing means possessing.

And so here we are, waiting in active stillness. Active stillness is the idea of action developing when nothing has happened yet. The mind knows, we all know, we are about to act. But first we must acknowledge the single-mindedness of the Radical-male who flattens everything beautiful in an attempt to accomplish one agenda: to rule. It is crucial that those who oppose these forces, and those who are directly targeted by them, discover, or invent, a core idea that connects all of the fights we find ourselves in. Like the body that is about to act, we have to fortify the connections, to assemble all of our scattered actions, to prepare for a single, sudden movement. It *is* one, single war, so it needs a single, unifying core to connect all of those who fight in it.

Yet we are ready. Being ready is an instant thing: it happens when there is no time to prepare, and what takes place is a swift transformation in our state of mind. The collective-female, acting as a single body, has already been activated to respond to the greatest ever attack on all that is feminine: an attack on our rivers and our air and our soil. From Canada to the Amazon rainforests, from dozens of Turkish villages to the British 'Anti-Fracking Nanas' who stopped an oil drilling company, from Kenyan forest rescuers to young female climate activists, all around the globe it is women who are leading the resistance to stop the Radical-male sucking the earth dry. They are protecting all that is fertile, just as they protect their bodies. They know their oppressors can be limitless in exhibiting brutal power but they know, as well, that strength lasts longer than power. And strength comes from the inside. They are here not only to seize power from the Radical-male. The female must replace domination with caring, competition with cooperation, and the plundering of the planet and humanity with nourishment and support. The female in the twenty-first century can replace power with strength. A moral revolution, if you will.

*   *   *

'Be careful,' says Asja, giving me the balance board. 'You'll be standing on an unstable surface. Don't do any of those funny arm moves. The balance comes not from the arms but from a strong core, the rest is a circus act. Focus on your core and make it strong. And look at a stable point, it's easier to keep your balance when you do that.'

The unstable political and moral surface of our times deceives us into making too many unnecessary moves. The constant expression of disgust over attacks from the Radical-male, the repeated expressions of shock at its greed, the endless loop of sharing despair and disappointment is neither active stillness nor the action itself. It is just a deceptive inbetweenness. It only unbalances and exhausts the core.

Elaborating on our differences and the distances between us – namely the endless culture wars over puffed-up identity politics – is nothing more than a 'circus act', like the funny arm moves that render balance next to impossible. We – men included – must come together in this business of building a female world. And a stable point to look at will certainly be provided by the joy of our assembled and connected action. United we will become a female Atlas, holding up the globe. But this time things will be different when our struggle is over. We will continue to hold it together *after* the end, we won't be ordered to go home when the dust settles. Because the world is also ready.

As the current system disintegrates, a power vacuum is emerging. If all that is female prepares properly and claims the future, from within this turmoil a new world can be built. The female, our Lady Atlas if you will, needs to lift up the globe and steady it to stop the concerted attempt to shake her off – this time for good.

My favourite exercise is the plank, and Asja knows why. The plank is about how much pain you can endure. That's kind of my thing. But then she warns me, 'Observe. Differentiate the good and the bad pain. We don't want bad pain. Only good pain. Good pain strengthens and corrects you.'

In these bloody times there are many storytellers trying to prove that avoiding pain is the right choice – the only choice, even. Not only that, they'll show us how to do it aesthetically. They promise to guide us to a safe haven in the current storm of pain, welcoming us to a serene mental shore, far away from reality. 'This is the way to survive,' they say, and some of us may even do so. Yet, centring life on the avoidance of pain means rejecting our instinctual craving for sharing. If you can settle for this morality of survival, go on then, settle. You will find, though, that it is the loneliest place and that it is *bad* pain, inconsequential and corrupting. A shelter is a narrow place in which you can only become gradually smaller; eventually your spine is folded and your circulation stops. The body is frozen.

Good pain comes from sharing the burden of our times. Doing what you can and everything you can to alleviate the weight for others certainly induces pain. Yet every ache comes with a true story, and vice versa. They are the shared stories that prove that we once passed through this earth. Without the ache that comes from sharing the load, we are unproven; a ghost ship sailing by at night.

'We want no stress on the face and no forced breathing. Make it look easy,' says Asja. This is what happens when I can't go on anymore, begging for the session to end through my heavy breathing. 'Take a break, and try again. And this time breathe under your armour.'

Despite all the enthusiasm contained in the statement 'a female world is possible', the struggle will not end when we can't go on anymore. We know how merciless fascism's bulldozer can become. I am not certain whether the young should be told the depths of evil that women have been cast into numerous times before. Chile, Argentina, Iran, Turkey, the torture chambers of the 1970s and 1980s where an equally brave generation was destroyed? But then, speaking of the fall does not prevent the fall, does it?

However, the façade we erect does matter. It is the image that those who look for inspiration will know and remember us by. Women younger than we are should not see us quail and therefore fear reality, for reality has never been altogether painful; the older ones do not deserve to be let down if we can't keep it together. We do not have the luxury either to dishearten the former or disappoint the latter. And if we fail we have no right to make an epic story out of it. How arrogant to advertise failure just because we failed. If we are to try again, we must breathe better this time.

Breathe under your armour. Don't hold your breath, hoping the toil will end soon. Live. Living – as long as you are alive – has always been possible, even during history's biggest catastrophes. Loving, laughing and gravitating towards joy are still possible under our armour. And those stories of joy should be transmitted to the young.

We must talk about the times when we breathed fully. Stories of how the joy of female dignity enlarges the chest should be repeated again and again. They too must know that the daily struggles of all wars are fought not for ideas or ideals but for friends, for the person fighting next to you. At times, it is only for them that you try again.

'Look, you see that?' Lately, Asja has taken pride in how my body looks, my new way of walking, and especially my form when I lift things up correctly. Now and then she shows me new muscles appearing on my arm or leg. 'Do you see this? This is new.' Still, though, I fail with the heavier weights. She pats me on the shoulder. 'We will get there. Be patient.'

The female, all that is female, is more patient than death. She is resilient enough to wait for more than two thousand years to blossom again. On 9 October 2020, in Israel, two female scientists succeeded in reproducing dates from seeds which were more than two millennia old, found in archaeological digs. Only one of the many seeds turned out to be female, but that sole female was very lucky.

The tree was called Jeremiah until it grew enough to show its sex; from then on she came to be called Hannah. The labour took fifteen years. The first small harvest of Hannah's fruit was celebrated worldwide. The 2,000-year-old lady was called back from the depths of history to be resurrected in our times with water, air, soil and determined care, alongside a strong faith in all these things – and in all that is female.

I told Asja about Hannah the tree while we were doing our balance poses, looking like two trees facing one another in the mirror while we each stood on one foot.

A mischievous spark flashed in her eyes. She suddenly stopped her tree pose, placed her hands on her hips, and asked, 'Isn't that a great story for that book you're writing?' Indulging myself in some pride for finally managing to interest her in a story, I gave her a cool nod. She said, 'We need more of those stories.' A few seconds later she finished her sentence with a serious face: 'Today, more than ever.'

Then we went back to our trees, two Hannahs standing next to each other, patiently keeping our balance in unstable times. 'Look at the mirror and fix yourself. Lengthen your neck and stand tall. I want to see some grace,' she said.

I managed to speak without giggling. 'Certainly, your grace!' We smiled under our armour together. The autumn light in the mirror suddenly seemed stronger.

7

Choose enough over less

In July 2020, as an authentic middle-class victim of lockdown, I reached a critical, if disappointing, moment in the new hobbies I'd been cultivating purely out of boredom.

It was my second Corona harvest, but all I had to show for it was one truly miserable tomato and a bouquet of premature baby rocket. The products of my two months' miniature farming were undeniably scarce; so scarce, in fact, that it didn't seem right just to carelessly eat them. So, I decided to indulge myself, and seek out some virtual applause on Instagram for my efforts.

As I gently laid my masterpiece out on the nearest sheets of A4 paper, to give my shared shots that perfect background, I noticed that I'd grabbed the printouts of this chapter's first draft. Next to the miserable tomato, the chapter suddenly seemed insufficient. My initial idea of praising the idea of less, that the acceptance of such an ideal meant a step forward into a better world, felt too naïve.

I was still the same at heart: 'a strong critic of Capitalism' – as they call me – and supportive of the theory that humanity should drop its obsession with economic growth, that the world can live with a less active metabolism. Like any other sane person I oppose the extractivism that carves out the planet's guts for raw material, and the rating of humans according to their economic merits. However, my initial enthusiasm about the economy of less was curbed by my Corona revelation, a revelation many of us had at the time: less was too slow and too little.

Once you become a farmer there is good chance that you will begin to think like a farmer. When not writing this book, my life was suddenly centred around weather conditions and the struggle against city wildlife – insects, crows etc. – to protect my five buckets of dirt, my proto-land. Although my life didn't depend on my farming, my state of mind wasn't too different from those whose eyes were always fixed on the horizon of the soil. Anything irregular was rendered terrifying; change meant potential danger. The image of millions turning to a simpler life of less, unlearning the sophistication that humanity had developed over so many centuries, suddenly seemed absurd. To begin with, less was not more, and it was simply not sufficient for our cerebral needs. The economy of less is an important part of the discussion about our future, but it is not enough to build a new model around, especially when the world is falling apart.

My friend Annelies was both disturbed and surprised on the day of my revelation. During our regular Corona Zoom coffee, she read me Virginia Woolf's diary entry from 26 January 1941, right in the midst of the Second World War:

> Yes, I was thinking: we live without a future. That's what's queer: with our noses pressed to a closed door.

It was an odd coincidence, because only a few days ago she had been making a similar analogy when describing the current state of the world:

> It is as if our faces are against the wall but because of the fog we don't know that we are about to hit it.

Two women writers, almost a century apart, feeling similarly trapped by the perils of their time. 'Your analogy is more fitting,' I told her. 'After all, Virginia apparently thought there was a door that might have opened at some point, but we certainly know that ours is a solid wall.'

In the summer of 2020, people were beginning to worry about the economic aftermath of the pandemic more than the rising death toll. The bored middle classes were finished with the bread-baking and tomato-applauding phase of lockdown, and most of us were busy protecting our small lives from the greatest ever crisis of Capitalism.

This wasn't remotely comparable to the destructive banking crisis of 2008. The current catastrophe was about unsustainable, grotesque inequality, impossible to fix with a government bailout. The structural failure was irreparable. The temporary Corona-induced halt to the global economy was not the reason for the crisis, but the catalyst for the disaster. Those who understood the economy, and knew the history of key economic indicators, were comparing the level of inequality to that experienced before the First World War. And unlike Mrs Dalloway, we knew that Capitalism had a habit of overcoming its crises through international conflict.

The problem was, the vast majority of people simply did not understand the ultra-complicated universe of the economy, leaving us with no way to describe the wall that we were about to hit, let alone plan to avoid it. Even for writers like me, whose job it is to understand and to interpret the fog, the vocabulary of the global economy was inaccessible.

'Right now, Piketty's thousand-page-long *Das Kapital* is under my computer, just so I can get that perfect Zoom angle darling,' I joked to my friend. Thomas Piketty's book, despite its weight, was a bestseller in 2020, for it not only proved that the system was not working, but also that we were running headlong towards epic failure. When she asked me if I'd read it yet, I was sarcastic: 'Well, probably it says, "it's the economy, stupid!"' And it struck me how we had for the most part become so nonchalant in our ignorance of the economy over the last few decades that, by the twenty-first century, we could hardly think of a solution better than recycling or buying organic to save the world from apocalyptic shambles.

I remember it was the mid-eighties when those with the best grades in our high school suddenly started talking about studying 'business administration' at college.

Even the phrase itself was new, and not a single one of us knew what business the course intended us to administrate. The phrase was part of the new enigma, in the same way digital technologies are today. Even pronouncing the words was enough to leave the rest of us behind, in the old world of the naïve losers. Those future business administrators, especially the young men among them, were behaving with the pride of an elite brigade, already conscious that they were bred to run the new world.

Then came the nineties. I was a rookie in a newsroom, and a new breed of journalist was beginning to emerge: the financial reporter. Mirroring the global race towards hyper-Capitalism and its behavioural culture, they were more like stockbrokers, the untouchables of the new world, than journalists. The way they talked about money was too complicated for us mere mortals to understand. And the topic of money was now synonymous with a discussion of the entire economy; it became something to be monopolised by those who not only understood, but also believed in, the game of finance.

Coverage of the other sector of the economy, the workforce, was now assigned to cub reporters, whose pieces would barely make it into the paper unless there was some big protest where people were severely beaten. The poor were irrelevant and invisible to the economics pages until they were killed, and even then they would only feature in a dramatic picture on the first page, illustrating the tragedy as if it were a natural disaster.

We were not stupid, we knew that it was 'the economy', but now the economy was nothing more than numbers, and the numbers were only talking to other numbers, not to us.

By the end of the 1990s the human aspect of the economy was entirely separated from the hygienic and numeric aspect, and had been exiled to a different section of the papers: 'human interest pieces'. Anyone who dared to mix the two was committing heresy.

There's that awkward air in the newsroom again. It is not the straightforward tension that comes with the classic warnings I have so regularly received. I know what that feels like, thanks to my choice of such prickly subjects as Armenian and Kurdish issues in my twenty-year political writing career. This is different.

It is a certain discomfort that makes you feel out of place. A sense of inappropriateness, subtly inviting you to be embarrassed. It comes not with the solemn frown that appears when we trespass on political or cultural taboos, but with the sour face of discontent, the muttering of vague words.

'These are really passé, sweetie. Why don't you keep doing that thing? What was it? Cultural criticism. And if you really want to write about other stuff, write human interest stories.'

This kind of vague disapproval only revealed itself when I wrote about workers' strikes. Writing about the 'underprivileged' and their dire living conditions was fine so long as you kept a pleading, sentimental tone. But portraying the lower class as an able force that could change the game of the economy was intimidating. Mapping exploitation, and hinting at a way out of it, was simply unfitting. The written word had to be *objective*, not 'propaganda', as I've been told countless times. Words had to be kept neutral in the power struggle between the oppressed and the oppressor.

The idea of social class was prehistoric, and so therefore were the tenets of Marxism that the Left had used to understand the world. For Marx, the material base (the economy, the production of goods, property) defined the superstructure (education, entertainment, social norms and the politicians who represent us).

Now the relationship between the two was reversed. We journalists, who had once focused our efforts on labour strikes or economic inequality, became convinced that if we analysed the superstructure long and beautifully enough through cultural criticism – preferably criticism of popular culture – we could affect the material base and alleviate the crushing pressure the economy placed on the most vulnerable members of society. Or rather, this was the only way for the dissenting voices of the time to be accommodated even on the periphery of the mainstream media, the amplifier of the new order. The poor didn't give a damn about our cultural criticism, yet we never ran out of topics in this new order of the world: the conflicts of ethnic, sexual and religious identities were everywhere, and they were more colourful than the fading, sepia images of class conflict.

It was like a secret contract: in order to earn a livelihood, dissenting voices promised not to touch on the fundamental conflict that the economic system was based upon, and as a reward they were allowed to inhabit the colourful ghettos of the world, the over-populated Soho of cultural criticism. And that was how many of us joined in building the popular progressive narrative that confined economic injustice to the human interest pages; the mainstream's occasional redemptive shrine.

Poverty was now a matter of identity and it had to be handled as such. And possessing the power of words did not change the fact that we were tamed consumers of this new world, not bold advocates of system-changing ideas. Thus we began dwelling in ethical consumption, a harmless sandpit on the periphery of the system. Socialist thinkers and economists were occasionally interviewed as village idiots, but our main job was to keep the popular progressive narrative fun and carnivalesque. The Left was globally defeated, and we were trapped in the crowded waiting room of history.

This forced ignorance came with two important consequences. First, the accumulated knowledge of the economy among progressives was erased from the memory of political activists, for it was impossible to transfer that experience to the new generation through popular Leftist discourse. And second, seeing and showing the blood and sweat behind the glittering system became exclusively the job of struggling NGOs, and those were mainly staffed by the educated middle classes. In the end, only a few of us remembered why talking about injustice, the constituting pillar of Capitalism, was deemed 'inappropriate'.

In 2020, Thomas Piketty, in the book which propped up my laptop (and which I did eventually read and admire), came up with the term 'Brahmin Left' to describe the well-educated progressives who had been disconnected from a working class that now supported right-wing populism. Many of us were masters of the vocabulary of post-modern theory, but the world of numbers, the very thing that ran and wrecked our world, was a foreign land whose language was gibberish.

And in 2008, when the global economy turned upside down, we had a lot of catching-up to do.

'Can you explain derivatives to me?'

To the mainstream, the documentary maker Michael Moore looked like a slightly irritating Leftist rabble-rouser, until the 2008 banking crisis. But once all hell had broken loose, an unprecedented number of viewers turned to his 2009 documentary to understand what went wrong.

In *Capitalism: A Love Story* he was asking a simple question and looking for a clear answer: what detonated the bomb that brought our houses down?

As he dug deeper, two terms in particular were unveiled as the sinister culprits: 'complex financial instruments' and 'derivatives'. Our lives as human beings were connected to these two phrases. However, only a small minority actually knew what they represented. Tragically, Moore found out that even the decision makers in the higher echelons of politics did not really know what they meant.

Moore revealed that the disciples of money were truly out of control, running the global economy as they pleased; and we, the people, were no more enlightened or less helpless than the medieval peasants growing tomatoes in their back yards. We badly needed someone to decipher the current complexity of the economy so that we could understand what to oppose. Yet we were too beaten up to understand or attempt to have a say, too exhausted to repel the inaccessible fog. Until something truly unexpected happened.

Certain challenges in human history require not a bookish political education but a massive crisis, or a dire necessity to broaden our political vocabulary. In such circumstances of urgent need for voicing our demands, the words that have been accumulating in history's waiting room suddenly become alive, circulating through our everyday lives. Almost miraculously people remember the words that will help them to resist, though they may not remember forgetting them in the first place. And that was what began happening in the spring of 2020.

... this conception of mutual aid is rooted in anarchist thought, which underscores the necessity of mutually beneficial reciprocity and independence from formal structures such as the police or local government. In that sense, Covid-19 mutual aid groups (CMAGs) work towards the achievement of a new type of society underpinned by collective solidarity.

In June 2020, Emma O'Dwyer, a senior lecturer in Political Psychology at Kingston University, wrote a piece for the London School of Economics website sharing her early research findings on over four thousand Covid-19 mutual aid groups in Britain. Although many CMAGs were built out of necessity, and with practical aims such as emotional support for the isolated, several such groups were already organising to solve their rent issues in ways that only a few weeks before the lockdown would have been considered the fantastical ideas of village idiots. As economic conditions became increasingly dire, these same groups, both in the US and the UK, began building mutual aid webs.

The 'losers' were developing resistance against landlords who held the oldest and the most untouchable pillar of capital: the land. For those who had witnessed the imposed transformation of these societies towards free-fall Capitalism during the Thatcherite and Reaganite era, the actions of these CMAGs were like a gathering storm against the shameless capitalist motto of 'There is no alternative'.

But an alternative was in the making, and an underground economy built on sharing and caring began to emerge. Out of nothing, and in just a few months, all while struggling with a global pandemic, people were organising. Even though many joined these groups because they simply felt the urge to help others, their basic moral intention enabled them to see that politics was an actual part of life, and that – once they dared to take a step into the manufactured fog of numbers – economics was something they could understand.

Being politically active suddenly turned from reciting Kropotkin's theory of mutual aid to being present at the small-scale, yet consequential decisions that are made in the real world, where that theory becomes practice. After all, it was not a specific political education that motivated people to have a say in the economy, nor did they study derivatives: the crisis of the pandemic necessitated that they show up at political meetings in order to democratise life, to avoid the wall that we all were about to hit.

'These transient solidarity actions do not mean much in the big picture of global economy.' As people dared to interfere in the seemingly unchangeable economic system, the same old, awkward discontent that I had seen in the newsrooms was already sticking its head out again with a sour face.

This was nothing new. For decades, one of the most common criticisms of those who held progressive ideas had been that they did not come up with solid proposals for the economy. And when they did, the snapped reply would always be, 'Not realistic enough.'

The progressives, having no say in the means of production, and having been mentally excommunicated from the realm of economics by the 'merchant Right', as Piketty calls them, for more than forty years, naturally seemed irrelevant to those who dedicated themselves to refuting all these humane and just proposals. They did not care about the obvious fact: in real life, the imagination is often limited by the thinker's means. Having been literally and virtually beaten out of the system, the progressives were incapable of coming up with a realistic enough plan to change the world. Imagining a better, and achievable, reality is only possible through understanding of our economic reality, and understanding reality is only possible by being involved in it. And only one year before the pandemic, such an involvement was the problem.

'A lot of people even like to feel a bit alienated by Capitalism – to not really understand how it works. They need to be reskilled, politically. Then we have to look at what economic powers they actually want.'

At the end of a long conversation about the new left economic movement, Johnny Gordon-Farleigh from

Stir To Action, an activist organisation, was telling the *Guardian*'s Andy Beckett that it all boiled down to whether or not the people were willing to enter the complicated land of the economy in order to change and democratise it.

A 'long read' about new left economics and its concrete achievements in the UK had centred on progressives' new interest in economic activism. The 'inclusive ownership fund' experiments in left-leaning cities like Bristol and Oxford were already coming to fruition, and local businesses run by city councils were thriving. (*Warning!* Since your eyes will have already caught the percentages in the following lines, you might reflexively skip this bit. Don't! We have to study this together, simply because this is our damn life. So, here goes. Inclusive ownership means that UK businesses with 250 or more employees will have to set up a fund, into which they will then progressively transfer 10 per cent of share capital, at a proposed rate of 1 per cent a year for ten years. The funds will be owned collectively by employees, with dividends paid on the shares being distributed to the employees, but capped at £500 a year per employee, with the balance being paid to the Treasury.) The proposal had become Labour Party policy, and the US presidential candidate Bernie Sanders had already adopted a similar plan.

The Left was making an attempt to disentangle the Gordian knot of our economic future. The idea of democratising business to regulate Capitalism had been practised until the end of the 1970s, but the courage to propose it on a national and universal scale in the twenty-first century was new. This was partly thanks to the widely admitted failures of Capitalism, a phenomenon that had even been documented in International Money Fund reports in 2016.

By 2020, the systemic failure was crowned by the pandemic; the British economy shrank by 20.4 per cent by August. The IMF was predicting that the deficit-to-GDP ratio in advanced economies would swell from 3.3 per cent in 2019 to 16.6 per cent in 2020, which in layman's terms meant that winter was already here and it was worse than the 1930s that brought the big wars.

Even the World Economic Forum was changing its tune. Suddenly their website was speaking a different language, mentioning the global need for a 'commitment to jointly and urgently build the foundations of our economic and social system for a more fair, sustainable and resilient future. It requires a new social contract centered on human dignity, social justice and where societal progress does not fall behind development.' So there was a very good reason for this welcoming mood for new ideas in mainstream thought, even though they might be hurting some capitalist hearts.

Unfortunately, even though this time the conditions were ripe for a *petit revolution* to democratise the economy, the general public was not as enthusiastic about having a say as many Leftist theorists would like to assume.

The four-decades-long pacifying of society, the effort to turn the majority of the working population into firm believers in Capitalism as the natural state of humankind, had been successful, apparently. Despite all the acts of solidarity emerging due to the pandemic, the general public were less than enthused when it came to claiming their share of power in the political economy. The end-times mood was so pervasive that many of us were already suffering from nihilism.

The Leftist proposals felt too good to be true to many of us, and it was already too late for the planet even if they were executed. I remember a black taxi driver in Washington who in 2019 told me he loved Alexandria Ocasio-Cortez, but wouldn't support her. His reason was she was 'too green'. When I asked him what that meant, his answer was quite telling about the general perception of progressive economic proposals.

'You know, rainbows and unicorns.'

Piketty, in his book, makes three proposals which do not at all have a sense of rainbows and unicorns about them: more extensive power-sharing within firms in order to establish true ownership; establishing progressive taxes on large fortunes to make ownership of capital temporary; and a universal capital endowment for each young adult. Piketty believes that the latter, which would be financed by the wealth tax, is essential 'if one truly wants to diffuse wealth so as to allow the bottom 50 per cent to acquire significant assets and participate fully in economic and social life'.

But then how many of us today are willing to 'participate fully in economic life'? To take part in the decision-making process in the workplace, and contribute to the complicated business of budgeting? Does our nihilism – be it the result of many repeated disappointments, or a learned reluctance due to generations-long depoliticisation – allow us to get up and shoulder the burden of transforming Capitalism? The question of our times will soon be this: are there enough people who are willing to join the game after all these years of being kept out of it, and especially when the game itself is falling apart? Can we transform the company, the clockwork at the heart of Capitalism, towards an entity with auditable moral responsibilities towards its employees that matter as much as the level of production and profit? Can we imagine and realise an economic policy that eventually removes the idea of private property and renders the accumulation of capital both illegal and immoral? And, most importantly, do we have the stamina to begin this immense work with small steps such as building a cooperative in our field of work, or strengthening mutual aid groups in our own communities? Do we have enough will to crack the wall that we are about to hit, especially when the sense of an ending feels so solid? After all, when we have such massive problems, speaking only of less seems not to be enough. But then what does?

By July 2020, every multinational retail chain had their own brand of disinfectant stations designed for their shop entrances. People were now able to carry out their Corona ablutions before entering H&M or Zara in order to bring back that lost sense of so-called normality. We were no longer guilt-tripping collaborators of consumerism. Now we had a mission: to rescue the global economy through our purchases.

In the new act of Capitalism, buying the unnecessary T-shirt meant protecting a sweatshop worker from starvation. So blessed was our crusade for the commodity that we suddenly dedicated ourselves to bailing out the sinking ship of Capitalism with our small buckets. Somehow, to many of us, this option felt more realistic than the rainbows and unicorns.

A particularly sentimental economic transaction took place in local independent shops. Buying less was suddenly a selfish idea when your local grocery was about to go bankrupt. Together we stood: the consumers as the terrified crew of the free-market economy, and the producers who were no less desperate than the second-class passengers of the *Titanic*.

We were truly left behind on our own when, in August, the eccentric multi-billionaire Elon Musk was bursting with joy after the *Crew Dragon*, SpaceX's first manned ship to the international space station, returned to earth safely. To many of us, his rocket looked like an escape plan for the super rich. And as those who certainly will not be on a spaceship to leave, our job was now both to democratise the economy, and to make a pact to regulate production, consumption and economic transactions in order to keep the planet and ourselves alive. What would be at the heart of such a pact? I began thinking.

'Happiness is the knowledge of having enough.'

At the end of Europe's strange Covid summer holiday, when we all began to realise the terrifying economic reality of our time indoors, I was reading Kurt Vonnegut's definition of happiness and asking the question, 'What is enough?'

As opposed to what many might assume, Capitalism does not operate in a closed loop of manufactured desire and the constant satisfaction of that same desire. In fact, the system operates with the fear of satisfaction at its core.

Capitalism has encrypted within every individual a belief that 'The moment I am satisfied, my existence will be invalid.' It is not the myth of happiness that drives us. Instead, the perpetual motion machine of unhappiness makes us active collaborators with the system.

Happiness is in fact a terrifying idea, and if Kurt Vonnegut is right, as he usually is, 'enough' is the enemy of this setup we are living in. Because enough is a progressive state of mind, allowing the individual to reject the system of greed in which the blind desire for more works as a constant attack on the idea of our happiness. We can always go on thinking about what is enough in moral and philosophical terms, constantly reviewing our description in order to devise some imagined better human, but enough is not only a transcendental matter, it is also a mathematical fact for the economy. It is a mathematical fact that has actually been put into practice in the real world. And I am currently living in a country where the memory of such a world is still fresh and tangible.

'We had less variety, but we had enough things.'

I'd accompanied my friend Merita, a Croatian journalist and novelist, to Emmezeta, a Croatian Ikea, to help her pick out a new bed. Since moving to Zagreb, I like to take any opportunity to ask locals about how the Yugoslav socialist model worked in daily life. The Yugoslav model is quite interesting, because it is not completely different from the system that Piketty and several New Left economists propose: an economy based on self-managing market Socialism, where enough is calculated by the people democratically.

Before the Soviet bloc collapsed, Yugoslavia had for decades been the hope for the rest of the world's progressives. In Turkey it was described as 'the smiling

Socialism', and was held in opposition to the horrors of Stalinism. But what interested me was not a bookish knowledge of the model and the intricacies of the economic system; I was curious whether it managed to define the idea of enough in the lives of the individuals living under it. There must have been a reason that the 'good old days of Socialism' was secretly becoming a popular topic in Croatia.

After searching through a warehouse filled with an incredible range of commodities, Merita and I stopped in the beds section and attempted to take in the vast selection we were presented with. Merita said to me, 'We did not have the current variety of things. But I don't remember anyone suffering because we did not have enough beds.'

And then she remembered a leather jacket she wore as a teenager at the end of the eighties: 'When we went to Italy for the first time, people I met were taken aback by the fact that I had an up-to-date leather jacket. They thought we all lived in Soviet misery. I remember feeling very cool at the time, showing off my Socialist-made leather jacket.' But then came the war, and then came the 2000s. Now the country has more, so less and less people have enough. As we walked around, breathing in that chemical smell of mass production, I remembered the stories of my country when we had been allowed to calculate the enough.

* * *

Women of her age, women with such an education, life experience and unfading *jeunesse*, would normally spend their time talking about their secret love stories or the things from their bucket list that remained unchecked. But whenever we got tipsy on Rémy Martin, her favourite, which I made sure to bring back from my travels, my mentor and late friend Demet, then in her seventies, would talk endlessly about the Turkish State Planning Organisation.

I was nineteen when I came across her, at the beginning of my first year in journalism, and the day we met she 'rescued me from the ignorant', as she would say. 'Sugar, the girl was in need of direction' was her favourite line when she told anyone else about those days. Until she passed away when I was forty-five and she was eighty, she never stopped transferring to me her knowledge of how to be a 'strange woman' as she called it, and still survive:

1. You have to know how to drink alone and not get drunk.
2. Be a great driver, because sometimes a woman has to run away in fifth gear.
3. Nobody has to know about your sufferings, cry at home.
4. You have to accumulate friends, not property.

There were several other rules, but the most important – and one that I never quite learned – was, 'Make a budget, you silly!' For me, money was always something to get rid of as quickly as possible, and so for years she kept reprimanding me, always ending by reminding me of 'The State Planning'.

Whenever she talked about it, there was a touch of 'We'll always have Paris' to what she said. Her Paris had been taken away from her by the 1980 military coup that forcefully transformed Turkey from a state-regulated mixed economy to a free-market hell. She could remember vividly the times when the country was run not by the haughty smile of the merry Capitalist, but instead by the concerned faces of the brightest Turkish brains, calculating for months what was enough for the country in every sector of production.

'This year,' she would shout suddenly, 'there are this many thousand elementary school teachers graduating, and the country needs only this many.' Or when the producers were burning their olives to dispose of the excess, she would almost cry. 'How could they not have calculated this already?!' Even when she was exhausted with cancer in her final years, she still had the energy to be obsessed and pissed off with the idiocy of the unregulated free-market economy. She even found the energy to read *Ulysses*. 'Sugar, with my luck, on the other side I will surely meet the writers whose books I didn't read. I cannot embarrass myself in front of Joyce, obviously.' The jokes were still her repellent against the pitying faces gathering around her deathbed.

After years of calculating and knowing what was enough, she left this world with a lesser heart. Many in her generation had believed that the science of economy could be managed towards a fair life, one that would protect human dignity from the attacks of the obsession with more. Even when her peers had been transformed into new people, adopting that familiar smile, she was one of the few who refused to join the game. When she died she still believed that enough is a mathematical fact, that it is common sense.

It was the world of indignity and unfairness that gave her cancer. 'It is all because of accumulated heart-breaks, Sugar,' she told me once. And by 2020, when that know-it-all grin faded away, even from the faces of diehard capitalists, her words had become fashionable enough to be articulated by the rulers of the economy. Alas, if she finds Rémy Martin on the other side and gets tipsy I am pretty sure she will track down Adam Smith or John Stuart Mill to torture them with her State Planning stories. Because she never forgets, and I too remember.

My repetition of 'I remember' when talking about the economy is not because of my limited vocabulary; nor is it the result of nostalgia. I want to hint at the fact that all the knowledge, experience and inspiration we need is already out there, in the past and in today's world.

What we all need is the will to step in and the knowledge of enough. And in whatever country you live I am sure you have brilliant projects for better economies buried in your history that you don't even remember forgetting, and that would give all of us enough will and stamina to try it again.

They knew, and we will soon remember, that the opposite of more is not less, but enough.

8

Choose the reef over the wreck

'The social democrats have been maddeningly incompetent. The centrist party is corrupt, and, if we're honest, actually quite right wing. And the new right-wing party is simply fascist. The new progressives, well, I voted for them but there's only a slim chance they'll even make it into parliament. Even if they do, I mean, clearly they won't be able to make any difference.'

I wonder at how many tables, and in how many languages, this lament for our political cul-de-sac has been expressed in recent decades. This particular example took place at the dining table of my Zagreb apartment in the summer of 2020, on the day of the Croatian general election. The short and strangely unenthusiastic campaign period had been barely visible on the streets, and my guests, all of them politically active people, were hardly talking about the elections. Around the leftovers of my Balkan-Mediterranean-totally-made-up fusion cuisine, a certain kind of weariness was expressed in a range of different words. Even if we forced ourselves to acknowledge the significance of elections, we could no longer consider voting as a constructive political action. It now seemed to be more of a desperate effort to prevent the worst possible option from being realised.

After the final drops of enthusiasm for the party politics of the 1990s had evaporated, the act of voting became the last remaining tool of democracy we could use to protect ourselves against a total lack of it. The ballot boxes were progressives' ever-retreating line of defence, and our votes were wooden swords with which to fight against the march of fascism, suited in full shiny armour. Occasionally when we had a hard-won victory, like in the 2020 American elections, our enthusiasm was so enormous that it looked almost tragic.

The people around my table had enough political education to know why those wooden swords had become so ineffective: if established progressive parties allow social justice to be compromised by unfettered Capitalism, then it's not possible to truthfully promise better democracy. And on that Sunday, we knew well that the issue that tarnished democracy around the world, could not be resolved by a few more progressive MPs making it into the Croatian parliament – or any parliament, for that matter. Until the core problem was

solved, the current form of democracy had to sugar-
coat itself to taste better, and use some virtual enhance-
ment to look attractive, in order to deceive citizens into
voting.

One morning Veronica Bielik, a young Polish woman,
woke up in her bed and found that she had turned into
a political figure.

It had only been twenty-four hours since she made
her first ever political Instagram post, and so far it
had received over 75,000 likes and more than 500
comments. Veronica had 2.9 million followers; her
profile read 'Fitness-Fashion-Travel'. Until her sudden
political metamorphosis in May 2019, she had been
advertising bold bikinis and extremely tight workout
outfits. But her latest, featuring a pose that centred
on her perfectly shaped voluptuous butt in sports
tights, was part of a political social media campaign,
carried out by Chase Creative Agency on behalf of
the European Union. The plan was to motivate young
people to vote, and the motto was 'If you give a shit,
give a vote'. So Bielik wrote about the matter she gave
a shit about:

Digital natives rejoice! In 2017 roaming charges
within the EU were eliminated. Roam like at home
means you're paying the same price for calls,
texting and data usage on your mobile phone

when travelling in another EU country as you do at home.

That cool picture you took for Insta on holiday doesn't need to wait for the hotel or restaurant WiFi to go up. I am happy to be able share all my insta stories from travels just during experiencing it. It makes all the emotions so real.

If you care about these things too, go and vote for the European Elections next week! #givevote.

While the EU was trying to make ballot boxes look sexy enough for the youth to bother voting, 1.4 million young people, the majority of them teenagers, had already been politically engaged enough to organise climate strikes in 1,400 cities around the world.

In the beginning, the action seemed like naïve young-sters worrying about the weather. But their demands were soon revealed: they wanted the total transforma-tion of the global economic and social system, in order to save life on earth. They needed no outside push to be spurred into political action. On the contrary, many of them joined the action despite substantial threats from their countries' establishments. Although their lives were shaped by this political action, they were not similarly excited about the changing of the guard in the political establishment, either in the EU or in their own countries. Expending their political energy through traditional political processes was not an appealing option. The climate strikers, and several other ongoing progressive protests around the globe, were deliberately distancing their political action from established politics.

By 2020, the establishment was looking more and more like a sinking ship – its efforts to build a better future swamped by the authoritarian wave. At the same time, the various attempts to find a new kind of politics outside the establishment proliferated, all in search of somewhere solid to land. Meanwhile on the outskirts of Europe a seemingly unrelated hub of life was silently developing.

In the summer of 2016, a junked airbus was laid down underwater in Kuşadası bay, a holiday destination on Turkey's Aegean coast. The idea had been to create a new spot for divers to explore, and, in time, the wreck would be accepted and slowly embraced by the creatures of the sea. The dead plane would accommodate life. The metal skeleton, this time covered with a different flesh made of a vibrating multiplicity, would revive. Eventually, it wouldn't be even called a wreck, but a reef. A new sovereignty would arise in Mare Nostrum, housing a multitude of living creatures.

Until recently the stories concerning this underwater attraction had been about how the plane was made to sink, but soon the divers would be telling tales of the octopus sprawling in the cockpit or the sea turtles making love in the business-class toilet. Eventually life would transform the skeleton, leaving no trace of the wreck. The schooling and shoaling fish that had been homeless would have a new shelter. And this is what politics might look like in the coming decades.

Since the end of the 1990s, those who act in, and think about, the new progressive political movements have been hearing and talking about the creaking sound of the sinking political establishment. But giving a name to the new political movements that have been circling around the sinking ship has not been easy. Thinkers like Antonio Negri and Michael Hardt called the phenomenon the 'multitude'. The French anthropologist Didier Fassin described the nature of these actions as building 'mobile sovereignties'. Whatever our choice of name, one thing is getting clearer every year: the intermittent yet continuous long march of the powerless has begun, and it is evolving before our eyes. A new political behaviour, and a vibrant soul, have been shaping among the global opposition ever since the anticapitalist Seattle protests in 1999.

The new progressive movements have been and still are full of seemingly impossible, yet invigoratingly fertile contradictions: they are powerful enough to alchemise the political atmosphere, but not really keen about taking power to govern the current institutions. After repeated disappointments in liberal democracies, they are not enthusiastic to become members of a political organisation in the traditional sense. They know very well that when there is no social justice, democracy is just a theatrical act, and that the social contract is nonsense when the poorest citizen is in no way equal to the richest one. Having lost faith in the institutions of such a system, these progressive movements are attempting to invent new ways to keep connected on a global level.

The agents of the new opposition are mostly over-cautious about protecting the boundaries of their individuality, but they can act as a perfectly synchronised and unified entity once the action takes off.

They reject the idea of a leader; either they bring out a new leader each time the movement is activated, or they attempt to practise forms of collective leadership. They take pride in being spontaneous and unpredictable, but so far they have a pattern: the physical protests appear like a reaction to oppression, but when they are met with massive state violence they retreat to their sleeping cells, rather than choosing to arm themselves as previous generations have done.

As a generation that has been born into an age of cynicism and sarcasm they are far from being naïve, yet many of them want something that others might find romantic: a benign form of power that does not corrupt, and a way to organise without the oppression of hierarchy. It is not a simple reversal of power relations between the oppressed and the oppressor that they demand; they are in continuous pursuit of transforming the very idea of power, both for global politics and within their movements. The American actor Harrison Ford was right to call the climate strikers 'a moral army' in 2019; their demands go beyond *realpolitik* and penetrate the realm of philosophy and morality, questioning the fundamental assumptions of the dominant system. The question of *how to be* is equally essential to them as the question of what to do and how.

As fertile as these contradictions may have been, they have also rendered the approach of the new progressives incompatible with the current institutions of representative democracy, including the established Leftist parties, and even more so the centrists. Even when the new progressives have decided to compromise their infinite colours to squeeze into the strictures of representative democracy, the conventional opposition parties have been unable to develop the organisational means to permanently accommodate them without decimating the dynamic nature of the movement. Since within the movement they do not follow the traditional rules of party politics, an organic mismatch has occurred whenever such alliances have been attempted. These two seemingly compatible Lego pieces do not click onto each other, whichever way they are pushed together.

It all has boiled down to one big issue that remains today: the new progressives had and still have a housing problem. They are not willing to enter the house of the establishment, yet neither are they keen to build their own home within the current rules of political structures – fearing that theirs might come to resemble the former. The resistance is simply homeless. They can *occupy* but cannot, or do not, settle down. Like the schooling and shoaling fish, they are searching for a unique construction that will not limit their wide-ranging variety of moves. A oneness is what they need, in which they all can sway in sync without any pressure being applied to those who fall off the beat. They ask seemingly impossible questions: Can we build a plurality without compromising the singularity? Can we create an embracing oneness that does not demand its components to be uniform? Can our shapelessness be a sustainable form? Can we reinvent a new politics that leaves no one out or behind? Because throughout the recent history of the movement they have seen faces that they do not want to forget. I too recall what they cannot dismiss.

'Stop silence, not life. In Croatia 90,000 people are suffering from anorexia and bulimia. They deserve free medical treatment.'

There is a man in Zagreb who stands in the city centre every Saturday with a big placard bearing these words. He does not shout or talk, but stands still with the placard hanging from his neck. He has been at this same spot since his daughter began suffering from anorexia years ago. It feels like he is waiting for something to happen, something that will remove his awkward loneliness. And whenever I see him, I am reminded of several other lonely faces in several different times and places. The old man in Cairo, on Tahrir Square, who had a big olive branch stuck to his turban. On his white dress there was a long written statement about the pain of injustice. History was being rewritten around him by an epic uprising, and it seemed he finally had a place to stand without being mistaken for the village idiot. I remember another man from the year 2002 in Porto Alegre. A middle-aged, local guy, who stopped by the political carnival of the World Social Forum (WSF) for cheap caipirinha but stuck around because of the heated discussions. I remember him almost crying when desperately expecting a 'yes' to his question, 'Is another world really possible?' Then a woman's face comes to me from India, Mumbai. She was a transgender sex worker who unofficially adopted a child. She was dancing with her boy during the closing ceremony of the second WSF in 2003, feeling perfectly included, probably for the first time. Her joy was pushing the limits of her facial muscles. Also those three homeless, glue-sniffing kids of Istanbul, helping their big brothers rock the police vehicle that was spraying water on them, all while laughing soberly and in full recognition of their historic role. The Gezi uprising of 2013 was probably the first and last time they were treated as a part of the people.

And whenever I see the man in Zagreb, the unforced moral and political ambition of new political movements seems more relevant and noble: including the most powerless, leaving no one out despite their irregular solitude. And when those irregulars flow in to be part of the 'multitude' they widen the limits of the movement, turning it into an infinite and amorphous architecture. This is the unique merit of these political movements; a merit they are not willing to compromise. Their ambition is not only to avoid excluding these faces per se, but also to uphold our right to be as irregular as they are. An inclusion that does not regulate: that is what they are after. This is the joyful humility upon which they want to build life and politics.

Structuring such an ambitious yet humble infinity is not easy. What kind of architecture can contain such volatile and fluid political matter without diminishing it? This new political magma searches for a container that will not resist the fluid, but instead will accept being shaped by it. And it will surely be invented. Until then, however, like all the homeless, the movement, the multitude, the 'mobile sovereignty' might need a temporary shelter in the junkyard of our wrecked institutions – not superficially, as in the EU Instagram campaign, but genuinely and organically.

This perspective might not sound revolutionary enough to some. However, considering the urgency of the Earth's problems and the imminent danger of altogether losing democracy to fascism, we may be obliged to incorporate our political energy into the conventional structures of politics in order to transform it radically, at least until the wreck becomes a reef. The octopus does not necessarily need to know how to fly a plane to occupy the cockpit. As Iggy Pop once sang in the film *Arizona Dream*, 'The fish knows everything'. And today the fish may even have a plan.

New York, London and Istanbul, three cosmopolitan cities that have always been the precursors of the near future of politics, were unprecedentedly rebellious in the spring of 2020. The governor of NYC was in the opposite corner from Trump when dealing with the pandemic, the mayor of London was in a cold war with Boris Johnson about the measures against the virus, and Istanbul's mayor Ekrem Imamoğlu was trying to keep the municipality's aid programme running during the lockdown, despite ruthless obstruction from President Erdoğan.

Several other cities or states in several other countries were in clear conflict with their central governments, each of which had been seized by right-wing populists. For the first time, the shamelessness and the comfortable carelessness that had become the political tools of such governments was being strongly challenged by the local powers in an organised and decisive manner.

As this moral and political tension accumulated, the residents of the three cities, for the first time in a long while, stood with their local governments, acting as committed opposition forces against the political insanity forced upon them by the centralised power. A new dynamic was emerging that has the potential to shape the political struggle of the coming decade. As if approving this new trend, local elections in France ended with the unprecedented victory of the Greens and Socialists, challenging President Macron, the man who had been elected as the last option against rising fascism. National representative democracy was paralysed by right-wing populism and the traditional opposition's desperate attempts to protect the establishment, but local governments were beginning to accommodate the new progressive politics. Local governments and the municipalities were beginning to look like reefs taking shape on the skeleton of conventional politics. This however was not news to those who had been in Brazil in 2002.

'Another world is possible,' shouted the thousands of people who had travelled from around the world to meet in Brazil for the first World Social Forum. Porto Alegre, the host town for the carnivalesque gathering, had been practising an innovative participatory democratic model combining the conventional representative institutions with the participation of open assemblies of the people. 'Participatory budgeting' was a process that each year brought thousands of residents together in public meetings to decide on half the municipal budget. It was the most successful alternative to both authoritarian centralism and neoliberal pragmatism at the time. The process was not only disabling the corruption that had infected Brazil's democratic institutions, but also challenging the poverty and inequality prevalent in Porto Alegre itself.

The model was proposed to the rest of the anticapitalist movement, but the resistance was then too confident to confine itself to municipalities. The massive defeat of the Stop the War Coalition, the synchronised worldwide protests against the invasion of Iraq and the complete lack of recognition of those demonstrations by those in power, had not yet been experienced. We all still thought that when people spoke, the authorities of the democratic world would listen. We were not fully aware yet that we, the people, were more powerless than we initially thought in the new, globally crippled democracy.

Today the illusion of having genuine democracy in an unleashed state of Capitalism is over. We are no longer watching the Rocky–Ivan Drago rivalry of the glittering 1980s. Today, on one side of the ring, stand the last mercenaries of Capitalism: the authoritarian politics that does not bother with democracy as long as the economic machine keeps working. And on the opposite side are the masses whose opinion is rarely asked, and only when a matter is inconsequential enough. Finally we have arrived where Porto Alegre had been all along. In the current dusk of authoritarianism, the municipalities are at last shining brightly enough to attract the new progressive movements. And it seems this time the new progressives are finally mature and experienced enough to change the shape of the wreck they choose to accommodate. Our political zeitgeist keeps telling us the same thing in different languages: the centre might be failing, but there is still a chance that the periphery can hold.

'It's delicious. What is this?' asked all my friends when I served the so-called dessert at the end of our democracy luncheon on that summer Sunday in 2020. Any Turkish citizen would laugh at their praise, for it wasn't even a proper dessert: a mix of roasted tahini and Turkish *pekmez*, thick grape molasses.

While we were dipping pieces of corn bread, the conversation kept switching from the general election to the following year's local elections. Each time the political possibilities for the cities were brought up, the conversation was refreshed and the possible local victories tasted better than my fake dessert. Suddenly, it was not numbers and the cold arithmetical face of *realpolitik* but the names, the people and the possibilities. Finally there was some political liveliness that I recognised from the nineties at the table. But then Mika, the evergreen killjoy of such sweet moments, asked solemnly, 'The centre can't be captured before the periphery is. But then without having the centre, does it really make a difference having the periphery?'

'Maybe,' I said, 'there won't be a centre anymore. Our current inability to imagine them doesn't change the fact that things can happen.' My enthusiasm was not because of the sugar rush, nor would I usually be able to resist Mika's appeal for pessimism. But it was only a few weeks ago that we'd witnessed something incredible.

'I am just so happy that I have lived long enough to witness this moment.'

In mid-June 2020, Angela Davis, the iconic Marxist and prison abolitionist, seemed as if she was answering me. There had been a question in my head for weeks: 'How does it feel for Angela Davis to see millions of people shouting her demands after so many decades?'

All those people like Davis, who 'had a dream' and sacrificed their lives for that dream, were now seeing things changing very suddenly. Almost overnight, their decades-long disappointment was to be erased. Minneapolis City Council announced their intention to disband the current police force, under the pressure of the Black Lives Matter protests that had begun after an officer murdered George Floyd.

Abolishing the police force was a slogan supported by a generation that had asked for the impossible. In the seventies, the Rolling Stones had sung 'Sweet Black Angel' for Angela Davis. But then the eighties and nineties passed. Davis was convicted in her own country, imprisoned and until recently demonised. Her personal history was the history of her generation: broken and suppressed. By the beginning of the 2000s though, we had entered a new age where the creak of the sinking ship became loud enough to be heard by all, and the new became visible to more people around the world.

Almost every uprising in the last decade that we consider a turning point in the history of the new politics had been impossible to imagine, even for the best political analysts, twenty-four hours before it began.

Nobody could predict that the Al Kasbah uprising would begin with one vendor setting fire to himself in protest at his poverty. He was not the first, and many thought that Tunisia would not 'give a shit' about yet another man burning himself to death. When a few dozen people began gathering in Gezi Park, almost no one foresaw that it would become the biggest uprising in Turkish history. Every big uprising that has shaped today's political zeitgeist began as if it were nothing. And we, who have the privilege of talking and writing about these movements, can only understand why and how they happened in hindsight.

To be honest, even those of us who had believed that there would be an outburst of anger at some point, were not bold enough to openly predict such massive actions would take place. We were no less surprised than Angela Davis, one of the most committed voices who once sang 'We shall overcome', when she said, 'This is like nothing I've seen before.' And we were equally suspicious of our skills for foreseeing political developments in our own countries, even though we assumed we had our finger on the pulse. This is the age, maybe, in which action surpasses imagination, and we may have to rearrange our understanding of politics accordingly. This is a different type of story, a story that builds itself before the words are there to describe it.

I am sure you've heard about the babies that try to enlarge the pictures in their children's books, thinking that the pages will function like smartphone screens. And kids are growing up with eyes already accustomed to watching 3D movies, whereas I can only take that much input for five minutes. Not to mention the virtual reality goggles that throw me off balance almost as soon as I put them on, as opposed to adolescents who are totally at home in that new world. It is a little tragic that, as a storyteller, I might have to surrender to the fact that there are now new media that call for an entirely different dimension of thinking.

Choose the reef over the wreck

One of my pastimes is to think about how I might write a script for a 360-degree camera; a story that has infinite openings in infinite directions. So far nobody has come up with such a form of story. The stories in this new dimension are still told in linear form: as the audience – or the participants – you are still directed to follow a particular story line, either by sound or visuals. Yet the camera is there, patiently waiting for storytellers to improve their skills. And maybe only those who are growing up accustomed to such dimensions will be able to invent that form of story in the coming decade. And they might, too, just invent the new politics in its quantum form. After all, this is the age of the unimaginable and the unforeseeable. But we have to be there not to miss it – so for now we might have to keep shoaling and schooling while being emotionally prepared to be surprised. All those dreams we had might not remain dreams after all, and one has to abandon cynicism to be prepared for those dreams to come true.

9

Choose friendship

'Get them off me.' I whispered the words at first. But Yurttaş kept taking photos until I raised my voice: 'Stop and get them off me now. Please.' Though initially hesitant, my photojournalist friend eventually snapped into action, and tried his best to be decisive when peeling the small children off me, one by one.

But when they began grabbing his arms and legs like sparrowhawks, he was as convinced as I was; these five-year-olds could tear a fully grown adult apart. He looked like Gulliver crushed with despair, swarmed by these attacking Lilliputians but trying desperately not to hurt them. The fear of hurting them accidentally, of becoming one of the evil adults, was so terrifying that his voice trembled as he tried not to curse, 'Get off me, you ...'

During the last week of October 2005, people in Turkey were stunned by a video leaked from an orphanage. It documented the barbaric and systemic violence suffered by the children. It was one of the caretakers who leaked the information, and on the night of the 29th that same caretaker was waiting for us at the door of the institution, bathed in mercilessly cold, white neon light. We sneaked in to see these traumatised children, whom the government kept from the journalists, hoping that the country would soon forget the incident if there were no more news stories about them. I was there to continue telling the story, in the hope that keeping it in readers' minds would force the ministry to open a proper investigation.

I always thought children and wildflowers were alike. Even after a long walk in the meadows, those flowers you pick, so transient they can't be identified by a particular name, are always ready to perk up and forget they are broken once you put them in water. Children, too, are always heartbreakingly grateful and easy to deceive into joy, I believed. That is why, that evening in the orphanage, neglecting my initial job, I wanted to offer these children some compassion, a drop of apology in the name of the adults. I had an urge to show them that not every touch hurts.

However, after only ten minutes of my naiveté they were climbing on me, pulling my hair, scratching my arms, grabbing me everywhere with their small hands.

It wasn't this unintended hurting that was unbearable; the real agony was my finiteness before their unquenchable thirst. It was as if they wanted to snatch away a piece of me; a souvenir of flesh to keep to themselves and suck on later at night when they became lonely. The caretaker stood there, doing nothing, as if she wanted us to see the depth of the matter, to catch just a glimpse of the insanity that can scare away even the most determined loving hearts like mine. Loving the loveless is not an easy job, she might have wanted to tell me, without saying a word.

At the end of the evening, while smoking in front of the orphanage, I saw Yurttaş – after all the horrid jobs we've done together in godforsaken places – looking broken for the first time. We were like two astronomers who had finally managed to peek into a black hole, and regretted everything they saw. The caretaker must have felt responsible for our despair. She decided to take a minute to join us for a sympathetic smoke. She said, 'They don't know what love is. I mean, they can't. Don't blame yourself.' Throwing her half-smoked cigarette on the ground, she walked back into the white neon. As the blackest hole in the human universe swallowed her, Yurttaş hissed curses of devastation between his teeth, and I was already considering leaving the children's grabbing hands out of the story.

* * *

Since the beginning of recorded time storytellers have been trying to convince us that human beings are like wildflowers; that a gesture of compassion can revive their innate ability to love even when it is buried in the deepest corners of their memory. Stories, holy or otherwise, tell us that if you speak the language of humanity it will eventually resonate with even the worst of our kind, to remind them what the essence of being is: the need for and the urge to love. When such hope is lost, they tell us, it is only temporary, a passing instant in our moral history. That is the job of stories anyway; they are supposed to prove to us that beauty is possible, especially when it is least visible.

Storytellers are the lighthouse keepers of history, signalling to us that the members of humankind, and their individual humanity, are not lost as long as they hold onto love's life-raft. But they rarely tell how much love is enough, or whether we have enough love in us to save one another.

Thus, in the *real* world, for *real* people, certain questions linger: at times when it feels like the dark matter in humankind has prevailed over our determination to love one another, how much love is enough to redeem our faith in love? Are we still capable of loving the human when he acts as if he has never known what love is? Can we redefine love in all its realness when everything about love seems fake, secondhand and cheap?

* * *

Whenever I need a holiday from 'our times', and I want to return to the early twentieth century, I stop by the old post office on Marticeva Street, in Zagreb. It is a place where the unfunny joke of life is on constant display: that those with the least time left are least able to rush. Thanks to the slow-motion old people, the only ones who still go to the post office, the minutes on Marticeva Street stretch out, and one has time to ask questions.

My favourite corner of the post office is the little book-stationery-souvenir-prayer-beads kiosk. It is run by an elderly lady who organises the newly arrived boxes non-stop: books published by normal people, for normal people. She sorts her peacefully unambitious stock into three sections: religious books – prayers mostly; cookery books – traditional mostly; and romance novels – written by Barbara Cartland wannabes, mostly. They all have wonderful covers: blurry images cut and pasted from random websites, and titles rendered in romantic fonts, dipped in all shades of pink. The kiosk is like a Rosetta stone for someone like me who lives for and with books, to learn about others who read to lighten up their lives.

On one visit, I am standing in my favourite corner, attempting to absorb the cumulative effect of these novels. I must seem lost, because finally the lady asks me in Croatian if I need help, and I reply in English, pointing to each book section, 'Eat ... Pray ... Love.'

She looks puzzled for a second so I translate, 'Julia Roberts!'

Behind her hesitant smile she tries to decide whether to repel the 'elitist' with a sulking face or to be dismissively polite. They call my number from the counter, so I walk away, very slowly, while asking myself why I am so reluctant to talk or write about love when it is as easy as baking a Croatian pie while saying three Hail Marys.

Love is such a loose verb that its object can be anything from shoes to God. The word can be spoken in the most solemn tones, but it may also be tossed around with the most frivolous giggle. For a storyteller the subject feels like putting an already chewed piece of gum into your mouth.

But love is so easy to talk about partly because we have hardly anything else left to discuss, at least not with the comfort we feel when speaking of this particular topic. When politics, science and all the other subjects related to the human condition have become minefields of polarisation, the word love seems to offer the only safe space for us to communicate without any danger of antagonism. In our terribly divided and unjust world the subject of love functions like a sandpit where everyone is allowed to speak and play without worry. Over time, we have become so used to being limited to and dependent on this sandpit that today, even the most epic dystopian narratives can seemingly be resolved in the final sequence by the same motto: love will save us all. Love is the multi-purpose handyman of our age. Or, at least, an equator-long, ocean-wide Band-Aid.

The hypocrisy of this abundance of love is so normalised that when people ask for their dignity or their equal rights, those in power react with surprise: 'but we love you'. And conveniently enough, when the hypocritical performance of love from the powerful is rejected, in our immensely unjust world any protest demanding equal rights, justice or dignity can be portrayed as the lack of a loving heart.

Think of the American cops taking a knee in the face of Black Lives Matter protestors. It was only logical and righteous for the movement to respond, 'Well, we don't want your love, we want justice.' This was read as 'black rage' by those who had been certain that love is the answer to all questions. Only hours later, those same cops where taking batons to those same protestors' skulls.

The tragedy is, our communication lines are so well calibrated to this 'loves me–loves me not' duality that even those who are aware of this miserable state of love sometimes find themselves 'liking' a photo in order to express their outrage over another black protestor beaten for demanding justice.

*　*　*

Thanks to extensive psychiatric research, we know that the real long-lasting damage to the foot soldiers of American colonialism didn't happen on the battlefield, it happened when those young men came back home to see that nobody gave a damn. Their minds could not cope with the fact that there are separate realities that one has to switch between with a flexibility that human beings cannot always manage. In some ways, in regards to love in the twenty-first century, we are all like soldiers constantly experiencing or witnessing a brutal war, but expected to be nice and conformist in another reality where everybody is all heart-heart-heart.

I am not just talking about those policemen who took a knee in recognition of an injustice they would soon help uphold. No, this mind-boggling prolonged conflict is more insidious. Haven't you ever had to attempt a genuine smile when you were thrown a surprise office birthday party, all the while knowing that those who were singing 'For he's a jolly good fellow' might be completely silent if you were sacked the following day? The job advert inviting you to 'join the family', with all its accompanying words of endearment – and lately even a couple of cute emojis – does not mean the love it implies.

This is what happens in a system where we have lots of love on the surface, but we all know that almost none of it is real. It is not the lack of love that is the problem, it is that other reality, the nice, conformist reality, where we pretend that there is love in abundance. That is why, despite the seemingly overflowing volume of love available to us, the world still looks like an orphanage where the loveless want to tear a piece of flesh from you. Millions of faces every minute of every day and night beg, 'Love me!' on screen, and the finiteness of the self is helpless before this massive demand.

So, the question is, as a person who happened to be born at this point in history, how can I love and talk about love in the midst of this prolonged conflict? Is it still possible to imagine human beings as friends, when having hundreds of Facebook friends passes as friendship? When friendship is a cover word for networking, the vulgar reciprocity of our business-oriented lives, where does that leave the ideal of love? And finally, when our smart machines can imitate the gestures of a caring friend while being ever-present companions, why would we still choose unpredictable humans?

The most important of all such questions is, can we still be friends, and love our friends, even when they appear so unlovable in myriad ways? Enthusiastically devoting themselves to fascist leaders even when there is no oppression; worshipping an economic system that is killing both the planet and them; proudly kicking refugee kids when nobody orders them to do so. Today the masses look like the hollow-eyed men at the Russian roulette table in the movie *The Deer Hunter*, searching for their soul in the same chaotic violence that caused them to lose it in the first place. Many of us have found ourselves shouting, 'Don't do it!' – to no effect. And sometimes it's even worse: our hollow-eyed friends take the gun from their temple, reach across the table and press it to our forehead, because we dared to speak of love as the true home while the bloodthirsty audience makes heart shapes with their hands.

The fact is, love reduced to such a banal level becomes the unwitting accomplice of evil. And if this distorted love is no longer fit for purpose in this turbulent age then we need a new kind of bond. The interconnectedness of the problems of our planet obliges us to imagine a wider connectedness among the humans that occupy it. But how are we supposed to bring friendly love into our public life without being sentimental about, and eventually disappointed in, our own kind?

'Maybe it is time we limit our relations to respectful friendship,' the young man said with his beautiful Middle Eastern street-smart smile. The conference room in Diyarbakır, a city in southeast Turkey where the majority of the population are Kurdish, burst into a supportive cheer.

I responded from the stage, 'That is a brilliant proposition. But then would we choose each other? Would you choose me? The Turk who has oppressed and exploited you all this time? I would definitely choose you.' Even though the subject matter sounded grim, the air in the conference room lightened immediately. Our relationship was no longer a burden of obligation but a matter of choice, of free will. Suddenly the words we began using felt fresh, which is quite rare when they carry the weight of a long and bloodstained history.

We were astronomers reminded that the universe is bigger than its black holes.

Apart from allowing mixed metaphors – as opposed to the stiffness of English – my mother tongue has another wonderful advantage for storytellers and poets: the Turkish language has no feminine or masculine.

The concept of 'brotherhood' does not exist. Instead there is a sexless yet definitely more poetic word like siblinghood (*kardeşlik*), which comes from the root 'sharing the same womb', but is not limited to blood ties. Like any other word in any language, *kardeşlik* has a layered history for native speakers. In a land where there are several ethnic minorities, hostile political communities and a long list of vendettas, the word is often used to conceal the unsolved conflicts of political history in order to maintain unity through forced sentimentalism. The idea that 'we are all siblings in this country' is frequently used by the dominant political power with an oppressive subtext, operating as a dog-whistle that calls people to submit to that common family code where the secrets of the past are supposed to be left unquestioned.

So the young man in Diyarbakır was in fact proposing a revolutionary opening to the political trap that my country has been stuck in for decades. On that day in 2010, the suggestion of friendship, as opposed to *kardeşlik*, sounded like a fantasy to many in the conference room. But today, when the hostile polarisation apparent in several countries has created new Russian roulette tables, it might be about time to explore the idea of friendship as a way out of our prolonged conflict.

The question of how we are supposed to love each other as fellow members of humankind has been troubling philosophers and political thinkers since Aristotle began talking about friendship. Spinoza took the ball in the seventeenth century and scored an epic goal on behalf of friendship in secular thought. In the twentieth century, first Hannah Arendt and then the cool French philosopher Jacques Derrida followed them. There have been and still are several thinkers racking their brains to answer the following questions: Can we imagine human beings as friends in order to create a better world and more humane ties for our kind? And if the answer is 'yes', then what are the constituents of such friendship?

There's hardly any need to point out that brotherhood has unavoidable hierarchies; that citizenship does not really hold water as it did before the 1980s when the idea of the social state was still alive, and when globalisation was not as obvious as it is today; that comradeship sounds ironically retro when used in today's sarcastic zeitgeist; and that identity-based community ties, after fulfilling their political duty, have expired due to their reductive effect on our political and moral existence. None of these imagined ties provide us with the wider solidarity that we need today.

Friendship, with its innate suggestion of dignity, the fine balance of distance and intimacy – and its ability to accommodate these virtues intrinsically – seems to be the only way to relate to one another in order to stay human. Considering that even the mention of the word as a political possibility can change one of the world's most ossified conflicts, as it did in Diyarbakır in 2010, I am hopeful that it can activate the joy of thinking together on a wider scale as well.

It is easy to adapt the question to other conflicts: Would an African-American choose a white cop? Would Algerians choose the French? Would the Windrush generation choose the British? You would be surprised to see the freshness of the air in conversations when the question is asked, for we all know that friendship is the ultimate and the most sophisticated form of justice.

Leaving the practical and *realpolitik* question of how to perform friendship in our public life in different contexts to a collective conversation that I would love to be part of, one point should be made clear. What stands at the core of such a wide-scale friendship is not sentimental love but a moral stance; a commitment to acquire and maintain a certain perspective on life and humankind.

On 22 July 2019, I was collecting stones with my mother on the shore of Lesvos. We were once again on the same beach for my birthday, a new tradition we established after I had to leave my country.

And in 2019, my birthday gift was two handfuls of heart-shaped stones. I still have them in my apartment in Zagreb. I keep them because they remind me of the conversation my mother and I had. However, some of those stones are not heart-shaped at all.

'What is the thought process behind collecting stones on a beach? How are you setting the standards? Why are you changing our standards after a while?' I asked her after noticing that the stones we picked had begun to look different to one another. She is a painter, and so the logic and meaning of shapes is particularly important to her, and yet there didn't seem to be a clear logic to which stones she was choosing. 'I mean when you start collecting, you decide to take only one sort of stone,' I elaborated. 'But then others begin to look somehow worthy of keeping. So what is it that makes us transform our initial standard?'

She said, 'I guess it's because you begin to see the beauty if you look long enough.'

Since it was my mum I could say what I wouldn't

174

normally: 'Or maybe the stones start looking back at us, so that we begin noticing them.'

We laughed, and my father made his classic remark, 'You two are not normal.'

To see the heart of the stone, or to find a heart in the stone, requires a way of looking that is shaped by loving attention. Not a judgmental look that weighs the value of the stone, or a scrutinising one that sees the unfitting aspects of it. What makes the stone 'look back at us' is that all-embracing attention that makes a certain familiarity in the stone suddenly visible.

Becoming friends is not so different. In the beginning, it is just a loose stitch initiated by a warm regard that enables the other person to look back at us. The rest of the relationship depends on what you weave together through words in order to make sense of the world and of each other. And in times of total nonsense – yes, there are such periods in history – the conversation of friends is still there to create meaning from scratch. When friendship has a solid foundation that allows it to mature, friends and conversation with friends eventually become the gravitational force in one's life. Friendship is the most profound confirmation of the individual as a human being. It is the confirmation that you are able to see the beauty in humankind and the ultimate recognition of the fact that you are, as well, a human.

If we enlarge this kind of warm regard to the scale of humanity we arrive somewhere very close to Ubuntu. The Bantu philosophical term became popular in the Western world through several African thinkers, the most recent of them being Desmond Tutu, the South African cleric and theologian. Humans are not separate beings, it says, being human is in fact a state of we-ness. It is very much like the friendly love that Western philosophy has been dwelling on since Aristotle, and the kind of friendship that this chapter is advocating for.

But then where does that leave my heart-shaped stones? Can a wordless being be a part of this process that makes sense of the world? Can it join the friendly conversation that constitutes this large we-ness? If one continues this train of thought one arrives at the gates of Spinoza in the Western world and Mansour Hallaj in the Eastern hemisphere, who was damned for heresy in Iran in the first century for saying similar things to Spinoza. The type of love that inspires oneness has not been and still is not appreciated by either the ordinary or the powerful. Yet, we still can and should imagine it a bit closer to today's reality and our day-to-day lives.

'I give up.'

Especially in countries where ignorance is mobilised and organised to become a political identity that champions the 'evil of banality', I keep seeing people, especially young people, expressing the same moral and political boredom, both on social media and in the flesh. In several languages, people who might once have been the pleading friend in our prolonged conflict are declaring emotional burnout before the self-assured ruthlessness of the banal and the vulgar that is coming from all directions.

However, as a storyteller, my role is to remind anyone who will listen that love requires a certain kind of attention, and that the easy despair of giving up on the human is a transient moment. Our never-ending job is to remember that loving other humans is not controlled by an on/off switch, is not a moment of spontaneous sentimentality. Loving humans is a commitment that calls for serious labour.

Poor Spinoza wore the same jacket every day until his death. The jacket was torn on the back, the result of an attempted lynching in Amsterdam that he barely survived. During his years of exile, he probably wanted to keep in mind what could happen when you attempt to become friends with all humans. Or maybe he wanted to show others the wounds inflicted by the darkness in humans. Yet his spotless faith in the word and his profound work on the idea of friendship is still insurmountable, telling us that the wounds that might come because of such faith are as nothing compared to the powerful ideal of humans being friends.

And Hannah Arendt, for her part, argued that such an understanding of friendship should be unsentimental, for she had also experienced terrible disappointment. Her love and mentor, Martin Heidegger, joined the Nazi party in 1933, the same year she was imprisoned by the Gestapo. This extraordinary woman had to think about forgiveness for almost thirty years, in the most depersonalised manner possible, while probably trying to overcome her very personal heartbreak.

For thousands of years, long before Jesus, those who spoke of the love of humans and the possibility of imagining all humans as friends were killed, tortured, exiled and damned by the political powers with the support of the cheering masses. This lovely picture of human history is so disheartening that one sometimes thinks that all those holy books preaching love and forgiveness are there not to cure the dark matter in humankind but to wish patience to the ones who are able to see the we-ness.

But the idea of a love of humankind and eternal friendship did endure – and so did the determination of those who voiced these ideals. The bloody endings of such historical figures naturally catch our attention more than the fact that they have been appearing and reappearing throughout history with unbreakable stubbornness. This persistence should serve as a stark reminder that the only support available in such a world, where one needs a lot of determination to continue loving humankind against all the odds, is friendship. That is the ground on which to confirm and reinvent the reason to love. It is the only place one gets rid of the hesitation to love and remembers one's own humanness. Only when such loving attention is directed towards strangers as a moral and political act, can one establish the bond that many people since Mansour Hallaj have died for. Only when one knows about the history of this particular branch in the history of thought does one realise the gravity of the matter, and one's responsibility to be a bit more determined for the sake of our late friends who walked this earth.

Also, to be disappointed in humankind is such a banal reaction, and such heartbreak requires no labour at all. To love other humans is not a broken hearts club; it is a philosophical and political responsibility that should be worked on with all the faculties of the mind, sometimes pushing our mental and emotional skills to the limit. It is a perpetual political action and a moral stance that is not for the fainthearted. It is the most serious invitation to challenge the bloody history of humankind. An act of resistance, if you will. And here's how you do it.

When you become a professional writer, whatever that may be, you speak more than you write. In our times, those in my line of work are expected to perform in various forms: solemnly and with a certain air of gravity in the Eastern hemisphere, and in the West with quick wit and lightness. So in Brussels in the autumn

of 2014, I was well rehearsed to give my usual performance with a woman called Annelies Beck.

'She is a famous TV presenter and novelist,' I'd been
told. 'She is going to do the stage interview with you.'
So when we began the gig I went through the Western
nice-person protocol; fine-tuned self-deprecating jokes
as the signifiers of humility, and the sprinkling of
compliments without too much enthusiasm. Overall it
is courtly manners modified for the twenty-first century
educated middle class. The only motivation that keeps
me intact through such nights is that I'll soon be back
in my hotel room, where I can watch an old movie and
go to sleep.

So, as is often the case, I was on autopilot when
Annelies said, 'So how about your mother? Although
you never mention her in the book, I felt like your
novel, *Women Who Blow On Knots* is actually about
your mother.'

My gulp was audible through my mic and the speakers on each side of the stage. In the prolonged conflict
of this world, who would pay such delicate attention
to my words? If I answer this very intimate question all
these strangers will know the answer as well. But then
how light her steps are as she walks towards the core
of my story. Can the curiosity accompanied by such a
genuine smile be so pure? Is it better to do my classic
moves of evasion? Is this another stone to carry home,
only to find out that it is not heart shaped?

I smiled a long, mock smile. She smiled back, and for some reason we began laughing out loud; a bizarre moment for the audience, but then for two women of inbetweenness – journalist/writer, professional/not really, pretending/not pretending, reserved/not really – it was risking the admiration of the audience for the sake of connecting with a total stranger at the deepest possible level, without knowing that it would hold.

In this dark space of humanity in which we had spontaneously coincided, we were now colliding by choice. Since that evening, Annelies and I have been friends: she is the one who saw the heart-shaped stone in me, and I am the stone that for a second was wise enough to 'look back' at her. And this is thanks purely to her taking the time to read me; not my books, but me. Thus have we two women established ourselves as a line of resistance against the dark matter in humankind.

It is time to go back to the post office on Marticeva Street in Zagreb to look at something that we might not have paid enough attention to earlier.

Yes, acting in friendship towards strangers, this truly pure resistance against the darkness in humankind, takes time and determined labour. The question is, though, can we risk being as slow-moving as the elderly people in the post office? Can we take the time?

My answer would be yes, because friendship is the only place where you can make sense of life at its true pace and in the native vocabulary of humankind. Friendship is the only space where our dignity and our ability to love are restored. But then we will all have to risk being perceived as just as boring as the old folk on Marticeva Street, and as naïve as those who came before us to start this resistance. This is the price one pays to see the heart of the stone. But it is, in the end, more economical than continuing to buy books on love by Barbara Cartland wannabes.

10

Choose to be together

'Since I began reading books I have become an unhappy person. Why should I read if it will only make me unhappy?'

Years ago, a very young woman, a teenager, asked me this seemingly philistine question. When her friends giggled as if they knew better, her voice crumbled with hesitancy. 'The words make life ...' Embarrassment prevailed before she could find the right word.

'Difficult, complicated, dark, lonely?' I asked back, scanning the audience to find her before she disappeared back into her seat. I made my guess. 'I would say dangerous.'

* * *

Words make life dangerous. Once they are out there to be read or heard, they do things to people and they make people do things. No word is too insignificant once it is marked into being through sound or letters. Those who work with words must be as careful as a chemist handling uranium or a biologist working with the Ebola virus. The dangerous nature of words calls for the utmost responsibility from the writer, especially when the words they're using have a blood-filled history. Take 'revolution', for example.

Lately I have heard many people say, 'A revolution is what we need.' They say, 'We need a system change.' I am dumbfounded each time by the ease with which these words are uttered.

Don't they know what those words mean?

It is not that I oppose the words themselves, but the terror that 'revolution' evokes, the chaos that 'system change' calls for – well, one must be ready to meet the impossible vocabulary that follows when such words take the stage. For it is next to impossible to come up with words that can heal the immense pain and the losses they drag along. Words, once mismanaged, have a habit of destroying lives. Only rarely can they make people happier than they were already.

I've seen too many young people sacrificed on the altar of big words. Brilliant university students relearning to tie their shoelaces because they're suffering from Wernicke-Korsakoff syndrome after hunger strikes that lasted too long; teenage girls whose faces melted in prison-riot fires; a Kurdish poet my age who went to prison because of a bank robbery when she was only eighteen, never to be released again, even though in the decades since she has only written love poems; young men who wanted to burn themselves to death in order to light the torch that wakes up the masses, only to continue to live half burnt – the list goes on. It was the big words they heard or read that activated a rebellion in them when the rest of the world was going about its business. When laying out the choices I offer in this book, I wanted to use rather more peaceful words – seemingly smaller and safer words – that take into account the nonchalance of the world they are spoken into.

However, I am not certain that any word is safe anymore. Because *now* is the time we have found ourselves in.

Now is the time that those big words will be called for, and it no longer matters whether or not we are brave enough to pronounce them. The 'system change' has already begun. The masses, long considered to be indifferent to politics and worldly affairs, are, globally, withdrawing their assumed consent from the system, either with a thunderous cry or through silent disobedience. Since there is no longer consent, the system calls for strongmen to protect itself, to hold the centre and use their limitless power to maintain rule. The moral and political insanity imposed on us from the higher echelons of politics is the consequence of this new dynamic.

This is no longer an abstract political matter but something closer to home, and more dangerous. We all know a colleague who is religiously devoted to a dictator and considers every critic to be an enemy of the people, or a neighbour who believes that the West should stay uncontaminated, or a fellow traveller who chooses not to wear a mask because he believes Covid-19 is a hoax, or a zealous pro-lifer waiting at the clinic door fully armed ... These crowds are gathered and mobilised by the strongmen, who have shaken the political and moral ground with their own sickly, powerful words, and created an unceasing instability. It is no coincidence that the dictators of our time are all giving the same message: 'If I go down we all go down.' A collapsing system is threatening to drag us with it, along with our faith in all that humankind has put together: all the moral, political and scientific consensuses.

This is how the new form of fascism opened, and will continue to open, a crack in normality, a state which had already been showing signs of wear and tear. Today, we can determine the direction in which that crack will spread by the words we choose to utter and act upon. Because at this point in time, despite the spectacle of the strongmen who have abducted our democracies, nobody is truly in control.

Choose to be together

The rule of law is disappearing, at different speeds in different places, and all around the planet the basic consensuses of morality are becoming a matter of personal choice. This is the beginning of a darker realm, where men eat men. Thanks to my country, which set off down this road years ago, I happen to know how it feels to be at the edge of such a crack as it opens, and what it is like to be constantly sucked in and spat out by a political centrifuge. But it is only when we are completely consumed by this perpetual madness, and the fear of what it could do to our lives, that rethinking our ideas about life, and what it means to be human, becomes a necessity. This book, with its ten choices, is my response to that need.

After being slapped, pulled, pushed and dizzied by this new form of fascism, many will find themselves in that lonely place where the insidious question materialises, 'Are human beings naturally evil? Do we deserve to exist at all?' In order to keep going, to keep ourselves humane, we will need to restore our faith in humanity.

Meanwhile it will become clear to us that the constant expression of anger does not change a thing in our political reality, but rather casts us as an ideal audience of fascism; exhausted by fury yet entirely inconsequential. In order to see and reverse the mechanism operating behind the spectacle, unceasing attention is necessary.

When we feel we are surrounded by organised and mobilised ignorance and that hope has disappeared it is determination, rather than someone telling us calming stories about hope, that will truly make us feel better.

As we see more and more people surrendering to cynicism, nihilism or retreating to their ever-diminishing safe spaces, we will need to keep the idea of friendship intact, not necessarily because we are sociable people but because we will crave to be understood and to understand. As polarisation and the collapse of institutions damage our conventional political and social ties, like citizenship or party membership, we will feel the need for a more sturdy connection to those of our ilk. When the dark matter in humans is invigorated with enough force by this new form of fascism that breeds and depends on violence and suppression, a new need will emerge to fortify the oldest word, a word that has survived genocides and world wars: love. Not the abundant shallow expressions of it, but true and determined human love. This word, after having been through all the troubles of human history, cannot die on us.

This will all be relevant and sound substantial once we acknowledge the reality we are living through: all the insanity of our times is the consequence of the collapse of a system, not the collapse of humankind. This distinction should be repeated by all of us until it becomes the zeitgeist.

All these humane words I've chosen to think on and to save from the current storm will have been to no avail if we do not do it together.

'I can't breathe.'

In 2020, these last words of George Floyd before he was murdered in a chokehold under a policeman's knee echoed around the globe. Although many Black people before him had died saying the same words, Floyd's last cry became the slogan for the biggest Black mobilisation in history. Apparently, the time had arrived. Meanwhile the world was trying to survive a pandemic that choked more than one million victims to death. Their dying cries were horrific and identical, 'I can't breathe.' Right before the pandemic, the young of the planet were already warning humanity, 'If you don't change the system, we soon won't be able to breathe.' And even before that, begging for breath had been spreading through continents for decades: refugees squeezed into meat trucks, people working in crowded sweatshops, the children trapped in basements during the scattered third world war that was happening in Africa and the Middle East; young women who are not allowed to leave the house; factory workers with scoliosis caused by denim sandblasting; white-collar employees suffering from sick building syndrome; and all those whose voices were deemed insignificant and who had forgotten how one only breathes fully when preparing to shout.

Many think that there are an endless variety of problems and that each of them calls for different solutions. But living in the age of differences, and overstating those differences, keeps blurring the fact: by now enough of us have learned what choking is. Isn't it clear enough that we are all negotiating with the system for a single breath?

I am looking for irrefutable words so that we can gather around them, and stand together during this negotiation with our times. The word democracy does not do the trick, and demanding human rights does not invigorate the masses as it used to do. Thus, I prefer to choose dignity.

We need words that are too close to the human heart to be alienated in our hazardous communication sphere, words that cannot be torn apart by political polarisation. These words must be as indispensable as breathing, and they must mean the same thing in every language. They must be words that we can walk behind together, as naturally and effortlessly as when asking for our right to breathe. And if and when we are put down, we will know clearly that our right to breathe has been denied. Only then, when the confrontation becomes clear, can we move on to the big words that evoke blood and pain.

Together, both as a word and as the title of this book, is a political proposal as well as a moral one. What I see in the world today is that the conventional political institutions are too damaged to offer a solution to the political challenges we are facing. Both national and international institutions have lost the last residue of their prestige, not to mention their already problematic moral high ground. Whatever we have witnessed as a positive political event in the recent decades has come from new political organisms, movements developing around the old ones or outside of them. We all know that these political movements have not sufficed to cure the system. However, they all have changed our perception of the world and ourselves. They have created new moral and political triangulation points to help us sense a new direction in history. They have neither been as decisive as penicillin nor as invasive as surgery. They have rather operated like antibodies, helping us to at least survive the disease so far. What is true of all these political events is that they happened when we came together.

Together, therefore, is the only word that might be dangerous that I am choosing to include as an ingredient in this new political and moral antibody. However, my choice is to no avail unless yours is the same. For it is, perhaps surprisingly, at moments when the word seems at its most dangerous, that coming together feels most inevitable.

* * *

Together

During the bloody year of 2020, when we most needed and lacked togetherness, something curious took place in each and every one of us, and it reminded me of my late grandmother.

She was one of the last nomads in southern Turkey and, contradicting her nature, she was married to a 'foundation builder' (which is the meaning of my surname today). As it became clear I had taken on some of my grandmother's qualities, she would tell me, 'The shoe that wanders too far brings back shit.' However, this woman, who owned a gun until her death, was secretly proud of my nomadic genes and the skill set that goes with it.

Nomadic or not, none of us were supposed to travel and come together during 2020. Coming side by side meant risking the worst kind of death. Yet our minds and bodies kept on rejecting this sudden change and many of us, risking bringing back home actual shit, travelled to come together, within cities and between continents. Each time our bodies leaned towards each other we had to make a great effort to keep our distance. Being on our own, something we thought we needed so very much, eventually became excruciating. During the year, many craved kissing, hugging or just being together with strangers in a crowded place, even if we knew that we might bring home some shit.

Together must be an archaic word in every language. It must have been invented to help us survive, or when telling the story of survival. The verbs that it evokes – to unite, to join, to gravitate towards sameness, to fit in, compromising differences while gathering – may sound far too outdated today. After all, humans have come a long way – from huddling our bodies together to survive a cold night, to travelling into space on our own.

Today we need the word less and less in our daily lives, in our studio apartments, in our cubical offices, at night with our headphones, in the mornings with our smartphones. However the milestones of life, birth or death still call for rituals that urge us to gather with others. And we still feel the elevating joy of oneness when an occasion for larger togetherness occurs, be it a football match or a protest. There is a certain kind of warmth when on a bloody Monday the train breaks down and we all sigh with shared frustration, or the extra indulgence we feel when eating in a restaurant filled with people. Many of us might have already realised how togetherness, even with strangers, has been an unnoticed necessity for all of us during the lockdowns of 2020 when we walked through empty streets. I probably wasn't alone in feeling like hugging the other regulars in my local café when the lockdown was over, even though I knew none of them.

In this new setup of carefully measured distances, the only happy faces have been those of the dictators; running a country is much easier when people cannot physically stick together. The greater body of the people have been unable, after all, to unite their voices against oppression, lies or shamelessness. Each and every one of us has acknowledged that togetherness is not only a physical or emotional need, but is also a political necessity if we are to be recognised as humans by the oppressive power. Coming together, we understand, is in itself an indispensable political statement. It is the only act or state of being that leashes the political power threatening to keep us in a chokehold. If we want to breathe, we have learned, we have to be together.

We have not said it out loud, maybe, but we have witnessed what happened: humans were forced to make a choice when going on to the streets for the Black Lives Matter movement, when Hungarians occupied the city squares against a dictator, when the Greeks walked together against war with the Turkish, when the rescue boats continued to sail in the Mediterranean to find the drowning refugees. Together has been our choice even when it was as shitty and as deadly. Masks worn, disinfectant in hand, off we have gone together to stop the political and moral crack from spreading in the wrong direction. Each time we believed in and trusted in each other with our lives against an invisible yet deadly virus. It was a negotiation with our times: either choke right now under the violence of the strongmen that rule our lives, or risk choking in a hospital bed later. That, I would say, was dangerous. Yet our faith in our fellow humans has prevailed.

I need no more than fifteen minutes to destroy all your remaining faith in humankind. However, attempting to restore that faith takes reading hundreds of carefully selected books in preparation for writing one, all while constantly experiencing an inner fight. Defending faith in God, even a century after he was proclaimed dead, is much easier than proving the worthiness of humankind as a dependable source of faith.

Religious faith presupposes forgiving God for all his injustice; however, a similar forgiveness for those who believe in their own kind seems almost impossible. Such an inconvenient faith it is, for it involves believing in and forgiving yourself.

While working on this book, in several letters to my close friends I wrote the same sentence, 'Ask me if I believe in what I write!' They mostly assumed that my remark was rhetorical: believing in our kind in our times seems like a joke, after all. It is not easy to inspire people towards such a faith if your own eyes are trained to see injustice, vulgarity and indignity when looking at the world. Add to that the fact that I have had a good part of my life stolen by fascism. The disgusting damage it wrought on my close circle gifted me with serious doubts about human nature. So why am I burdening myself with this matter of faith?

After giving a lot of thought to this very personal yet political question that had busied people like me for centuries, I finally came up with a simple answer, one no less personal or political than the question itself: I want to be free, therefore I want to forgive my kind – myself not excluded.

However, like many others who are no less inquisitive than me, I need solid reasons to forgive. As opposed to religious belief, believing in humankind is not a self-evident loop that begins and ends in itself. It has to be more than a divine tautology. It should be something more than *because it is*. And *I* have to be more than this. I personally – and politically – chose to write this book to be free and to be *more*.

I have seen several old people, mostly women, leave this world feeling that life was indebted to them. They were political and virtuous people, who believed that humankind could be better, do better, and dedicated their time on earth to make it so. But as they aged, as they saw all the evil and the vulgarity of their own kind in today's world, their faith was broken.

Faith – they might have grown too tired to remember this – is of no use to its object. Instead it heals the one who believes, who needs to believe.

I wrote this book to heal myself after seeing all the things I have seen, which I assume were no less disgusting nor more wondrous than what you are going through today. I don't want to die feeling that the world owes me. This book is my solid reason to forgive my own kind; a testimony to remind myself in times of doubt that I have to sustain my passion for infatuation with my own kind for my own sake. This is an attempt to protect my own joy of life. *I was* after all, and *I am.* And it takes writing a book titled *Together* to say, *I will be.*

It is a dangerous sentence, but it is the most freeing. So hereby, I choose to say:

I believe in you. You were. You are. And we will, together, be.

My thanks to

Helen Garnons-Williams, a *perfect day for bananafish* and I simply love you.

Jordan Mulligan, you are a special person and soon many people will be repeating this fact. Period.

Robert Caskie, I now know: what I want may not be what I need.

Daniel Thrilling, thank you for your patience with my grammar.

My wonder-women; Burçak, Ayşe, Shegül, Aylin, Selen, Annelies, Mika, Petra, Asja, Mateja … Thank you for protecting me from myself with your effortlessly used superpowers.

And of course Umut, always.

Also, Ante, thank you for lighting up my stove every winter.